The Bridge of Flowers in Shelburne Falls

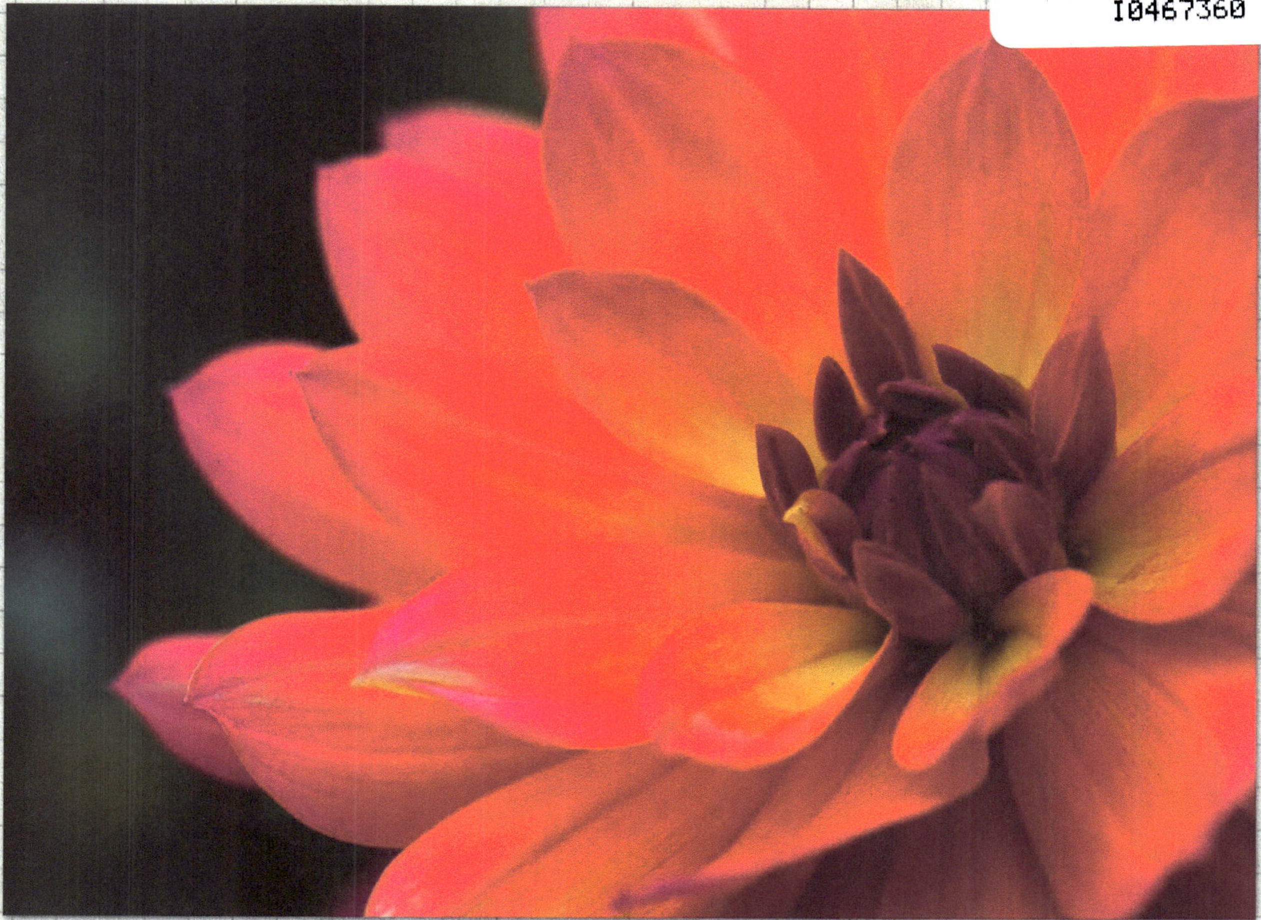

by Kathleen Odenthal

The Bridge of Flowers
Located in Shelburne Falls

The famous Bridge of Flowers is the only one of its kind in the entire world. Built in 1908 as a trolley bridge across the Deerfield Rivr, connecting the towns of Shelburne and Bucland, the bridge is 400 feet long with five archways along the path.

In 1929 the bridge was transformed into the flower bridge by Antoinette and Walter Burnham. Spearheaded by the Shelburne Falls Woman's Club, the bridge continues to be well maintained and draws in people from all over the globe.

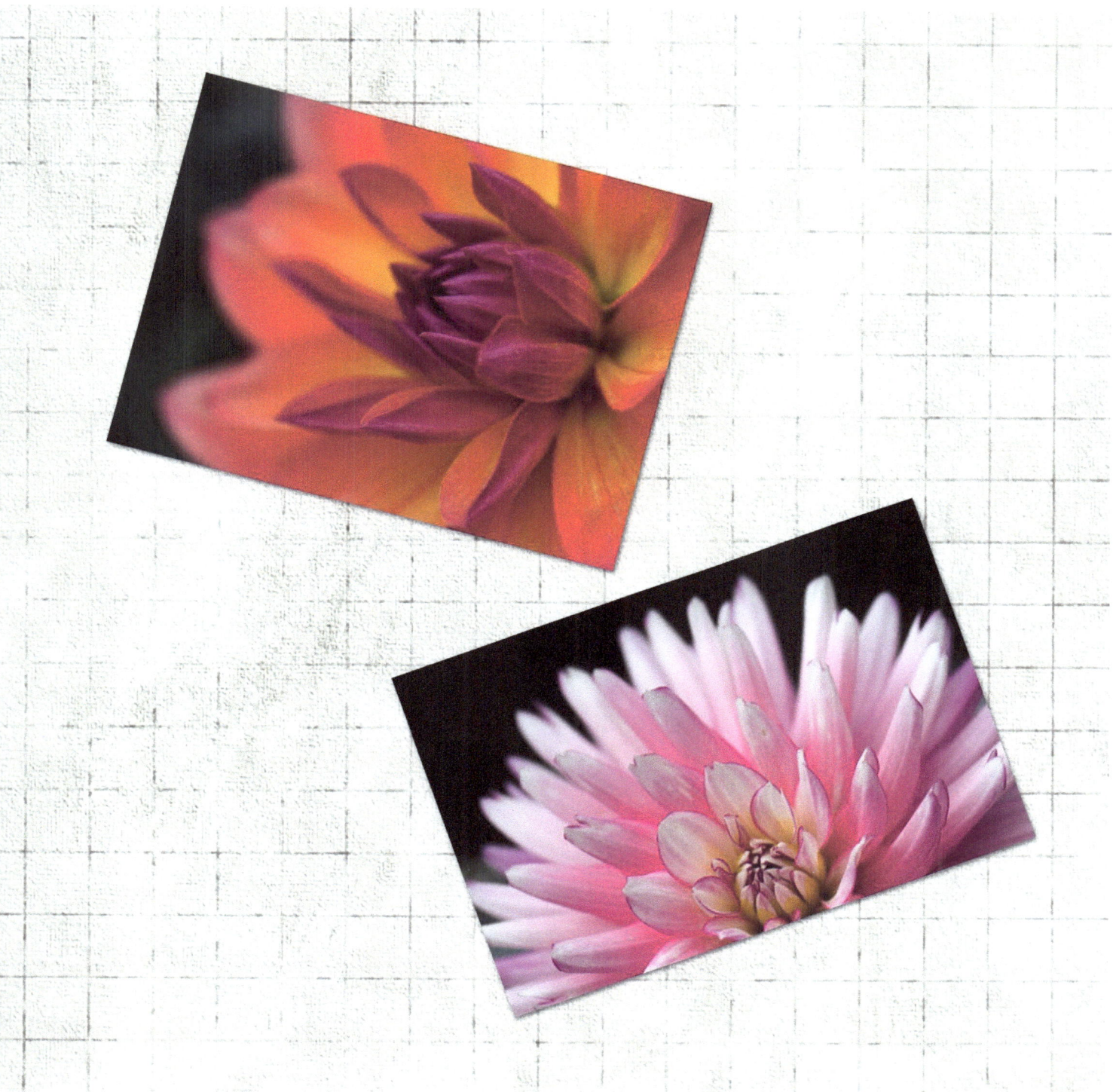

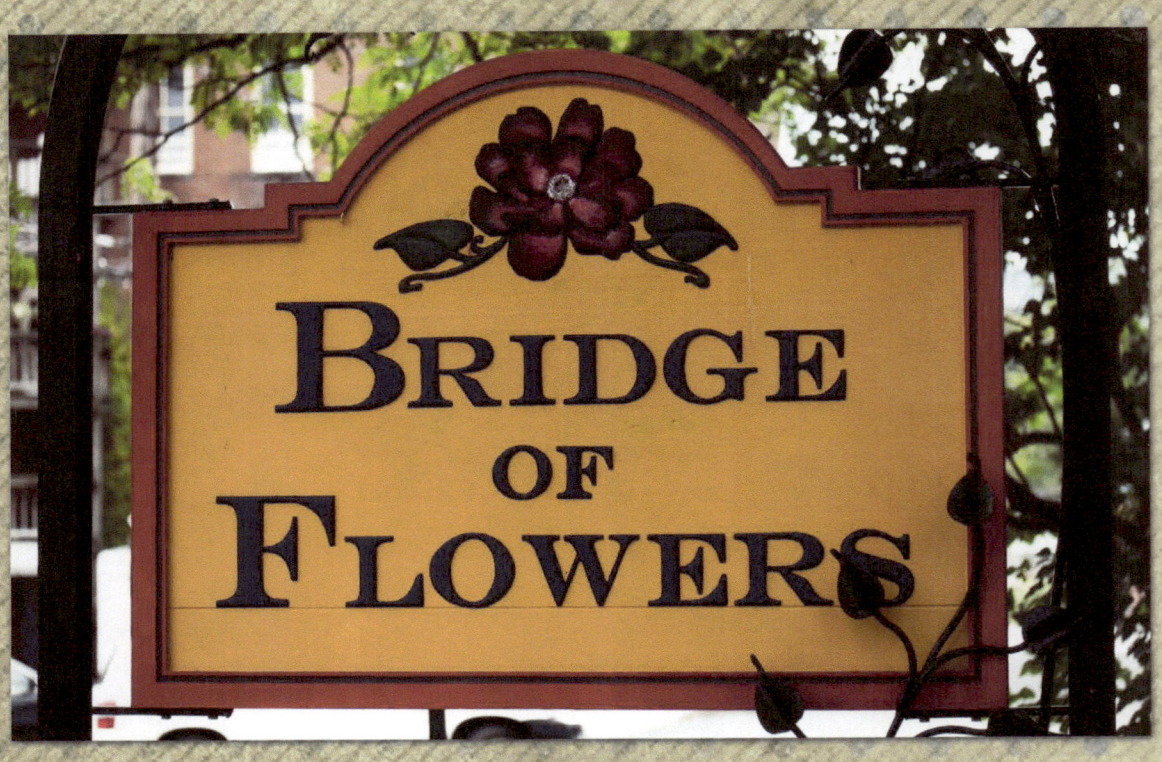

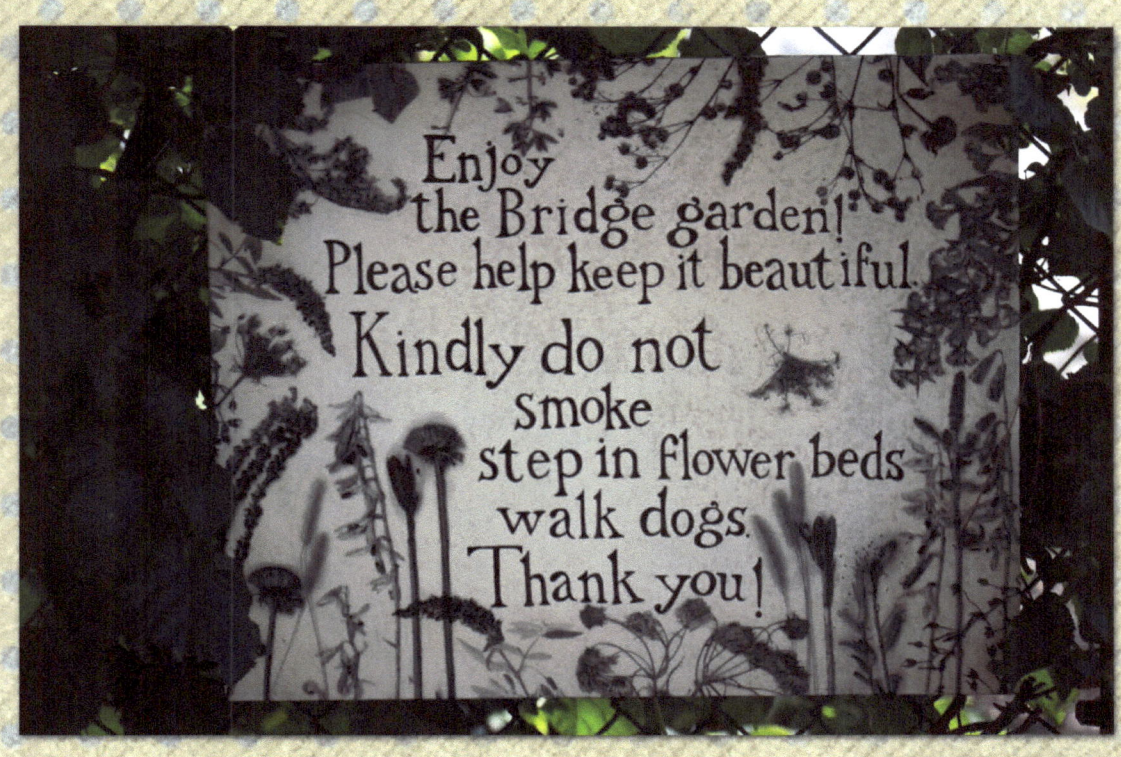

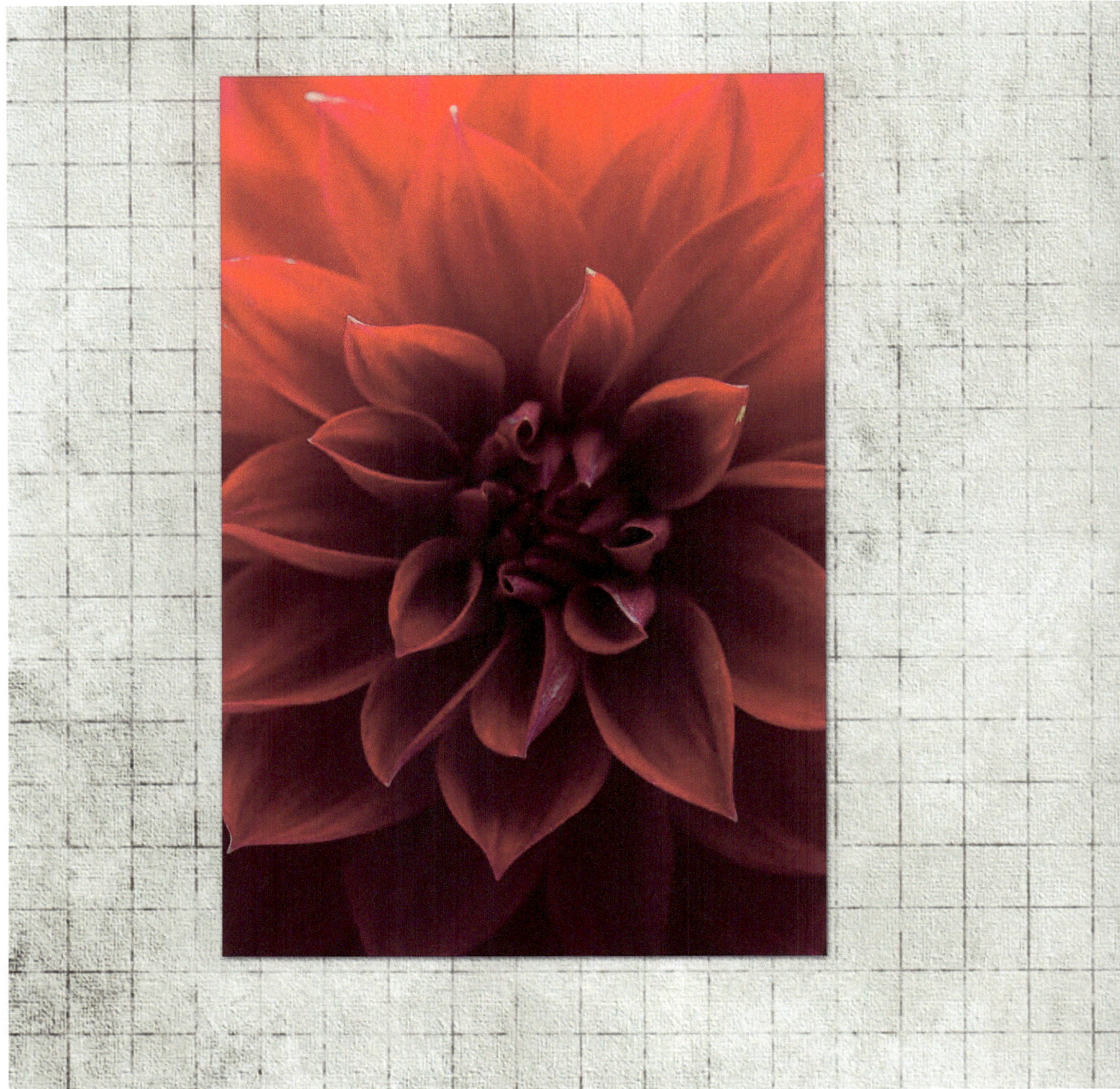

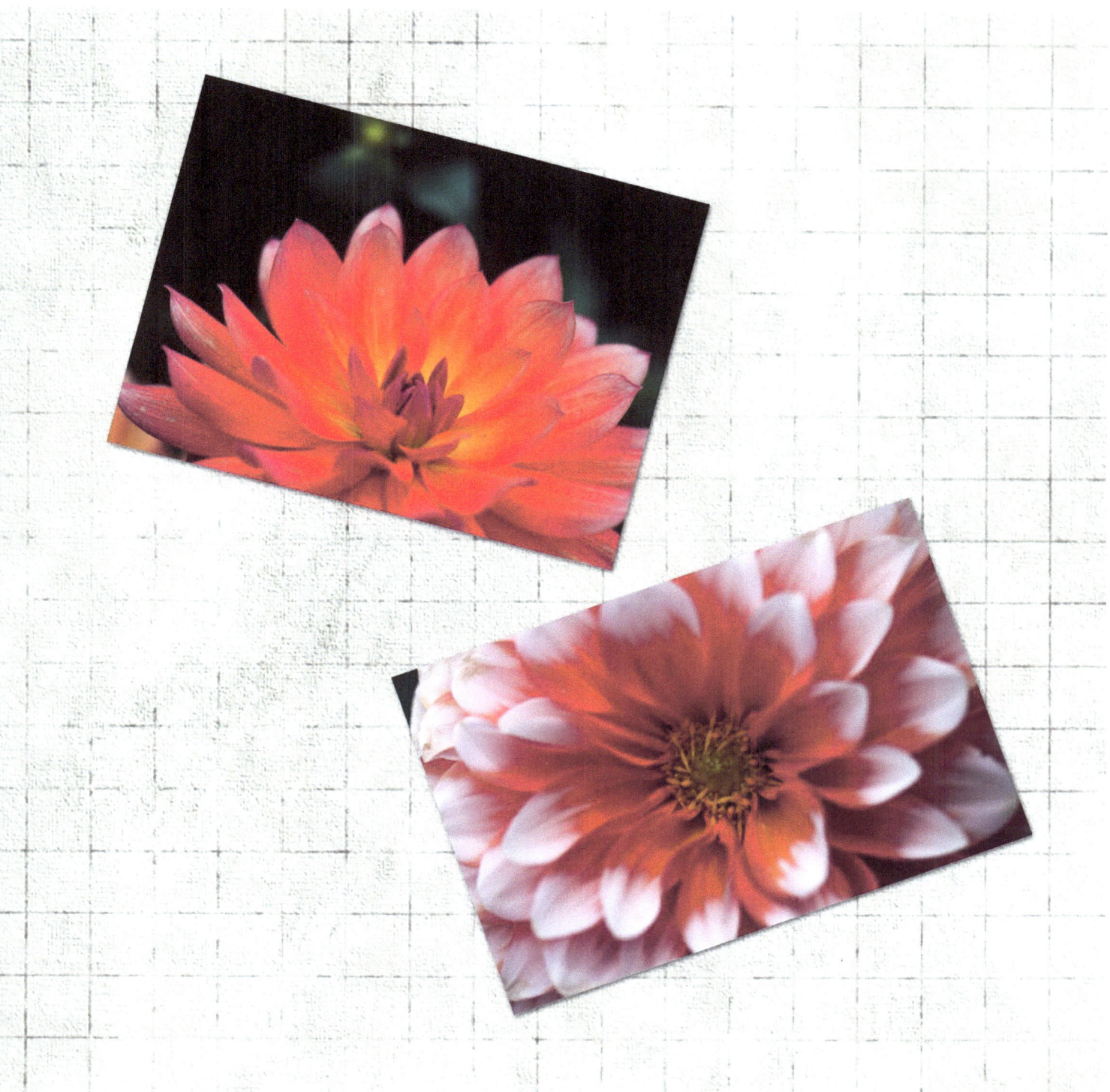

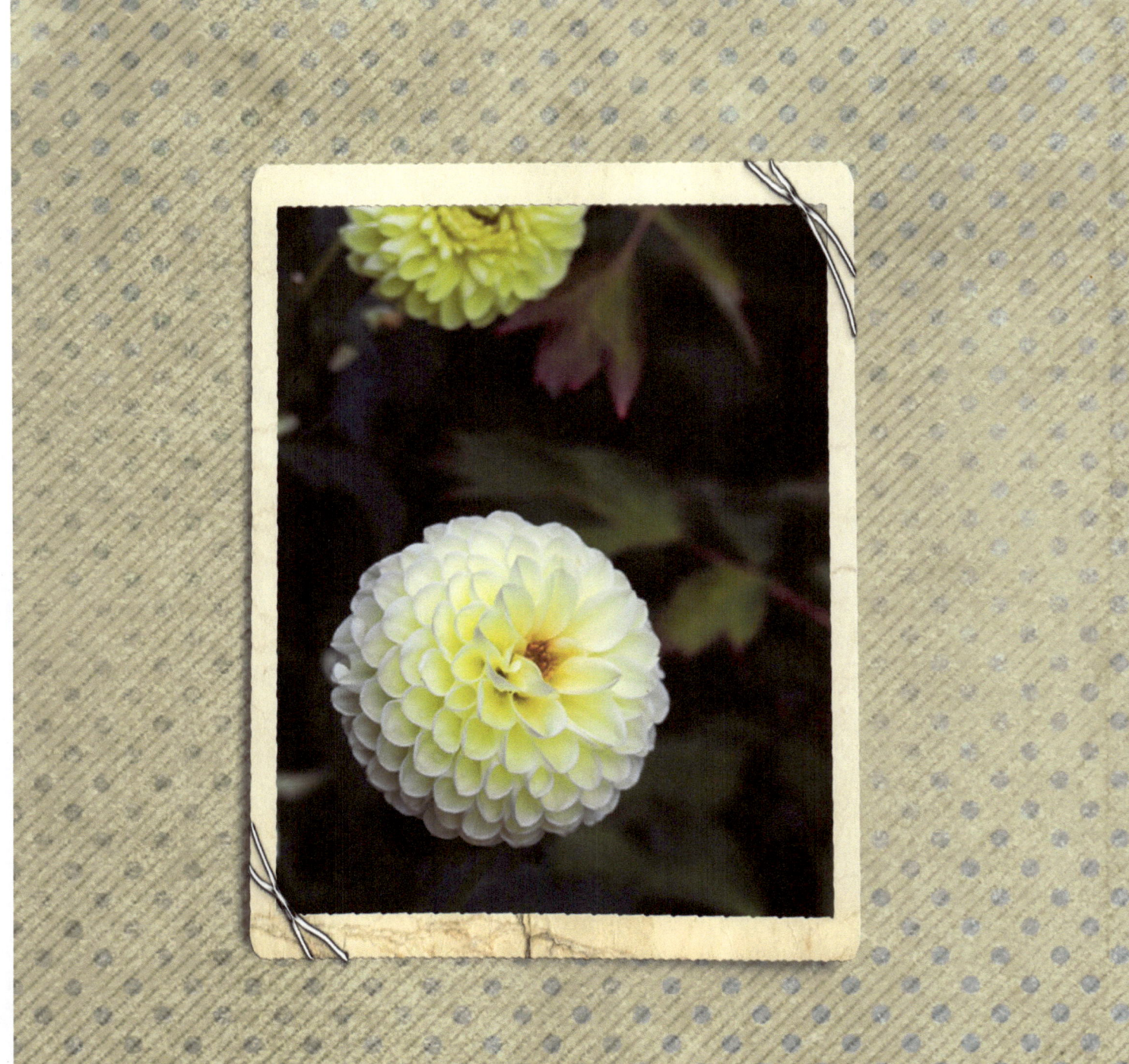

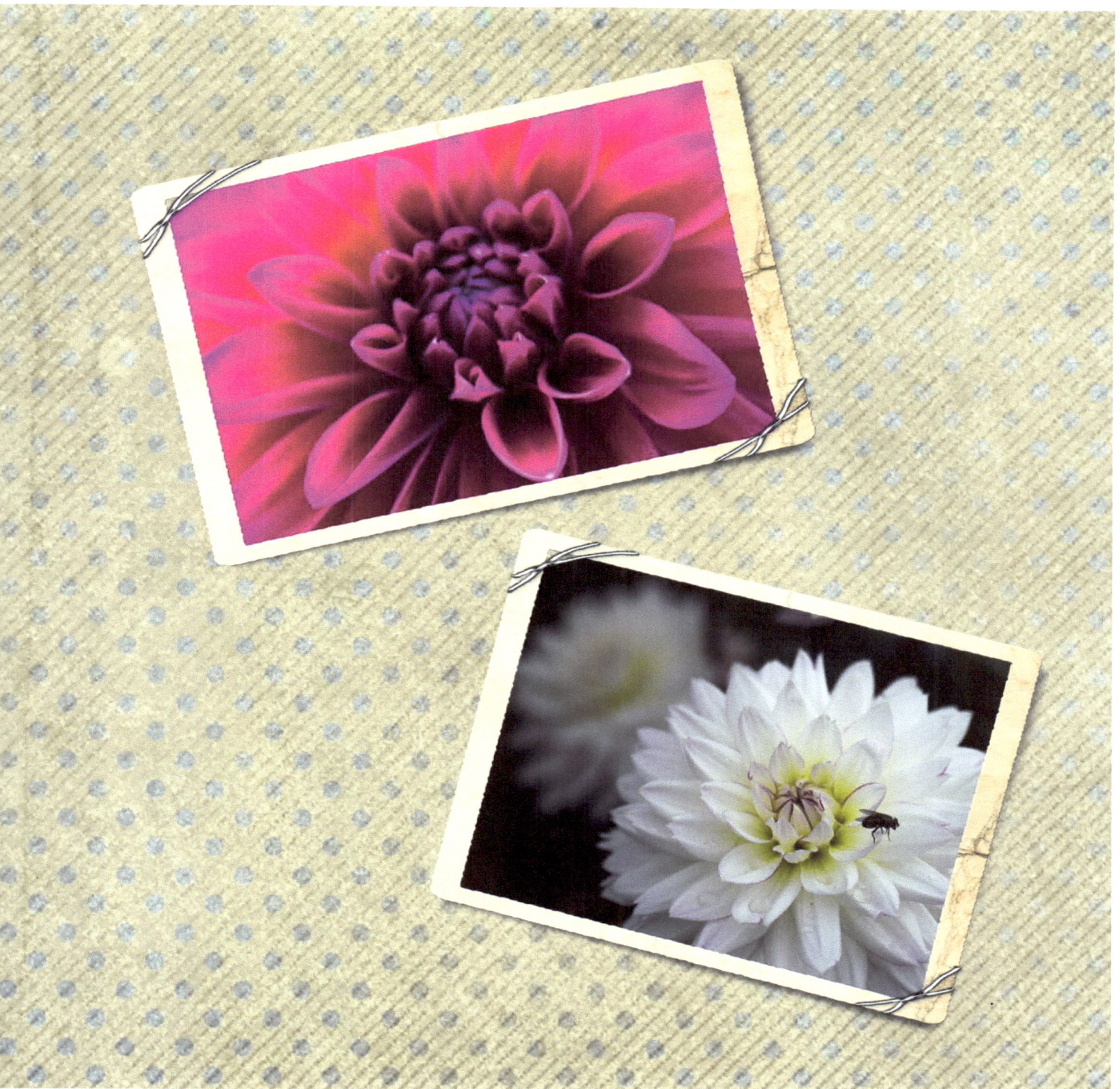

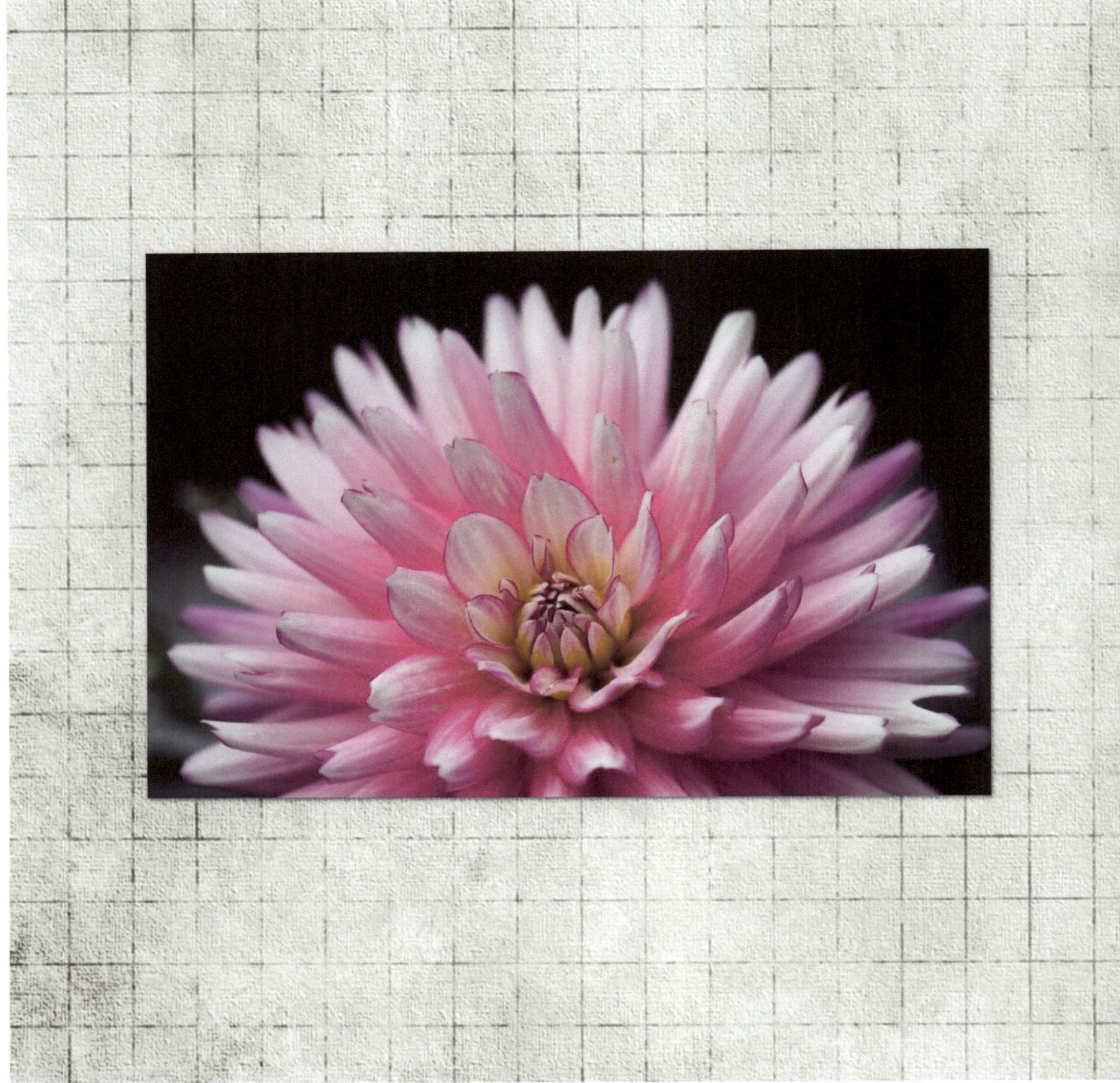

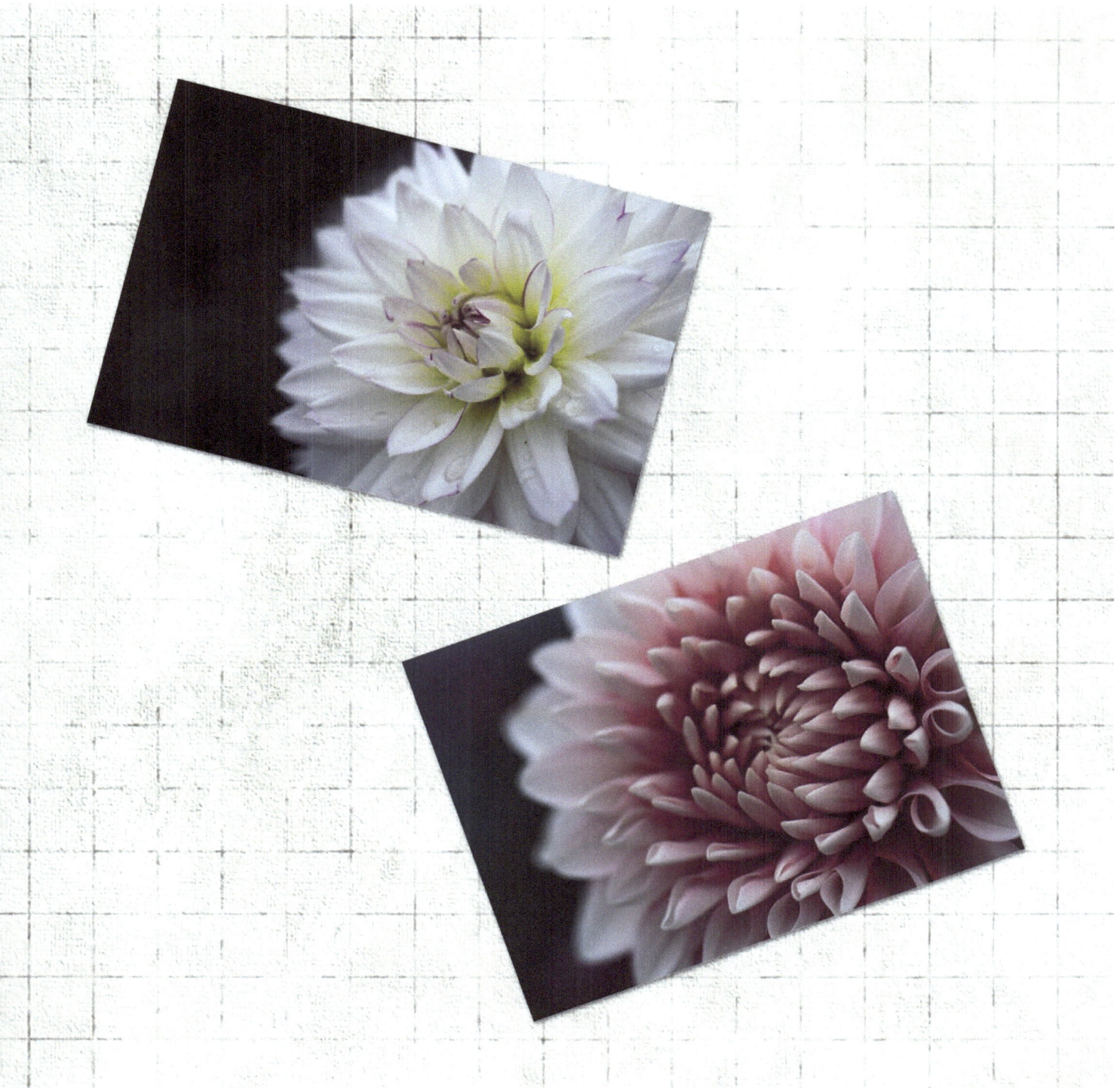

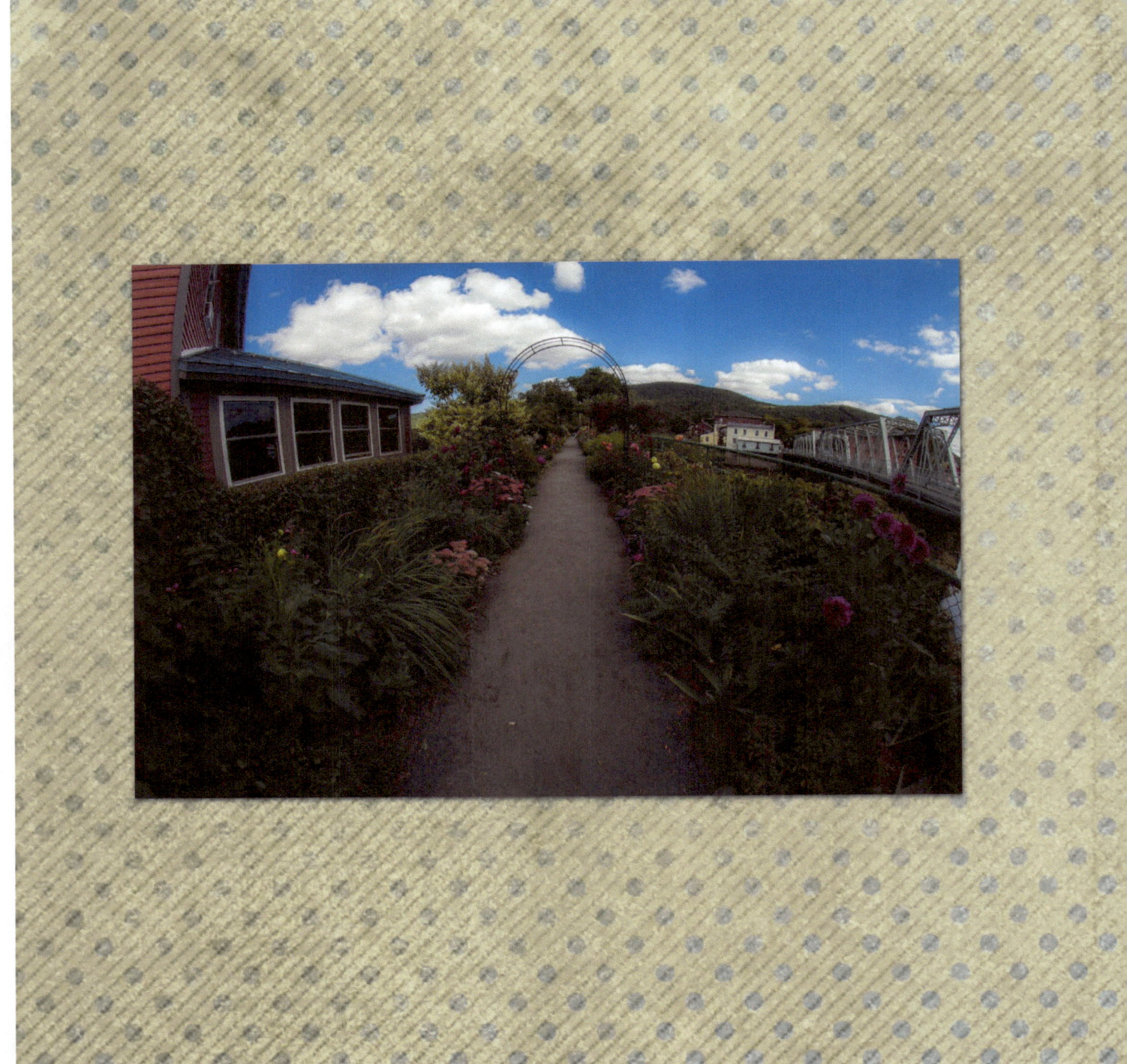

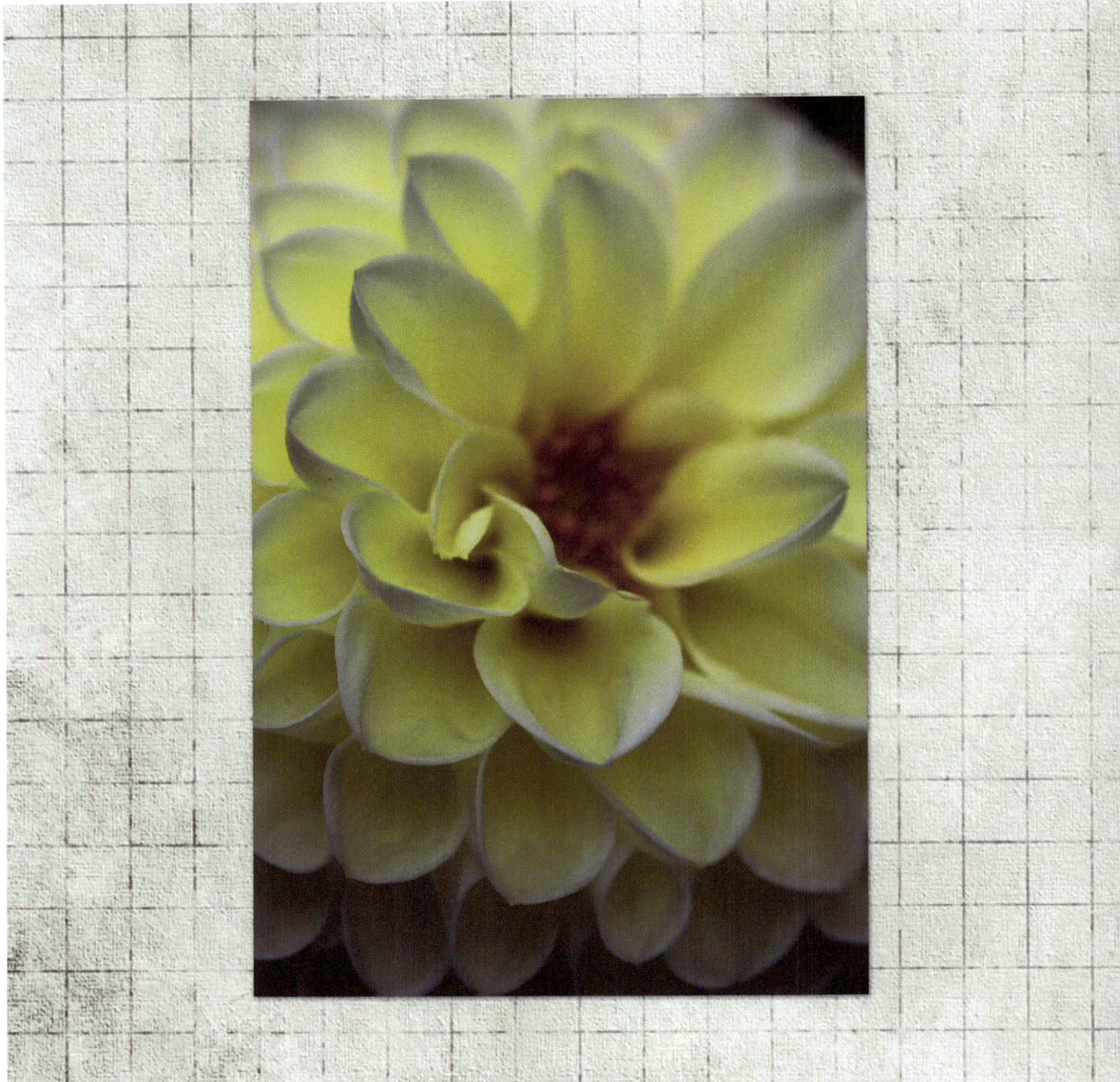

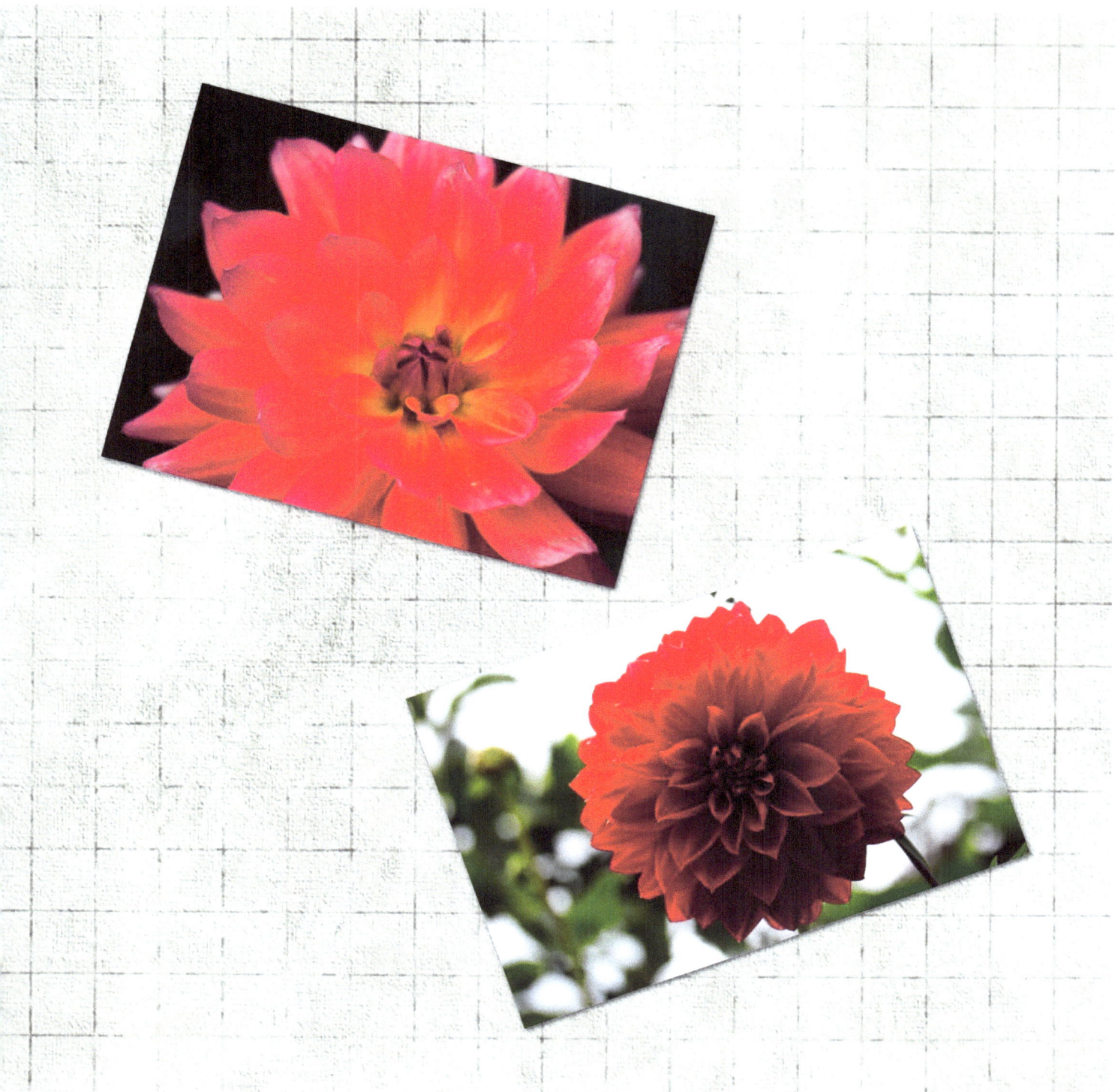

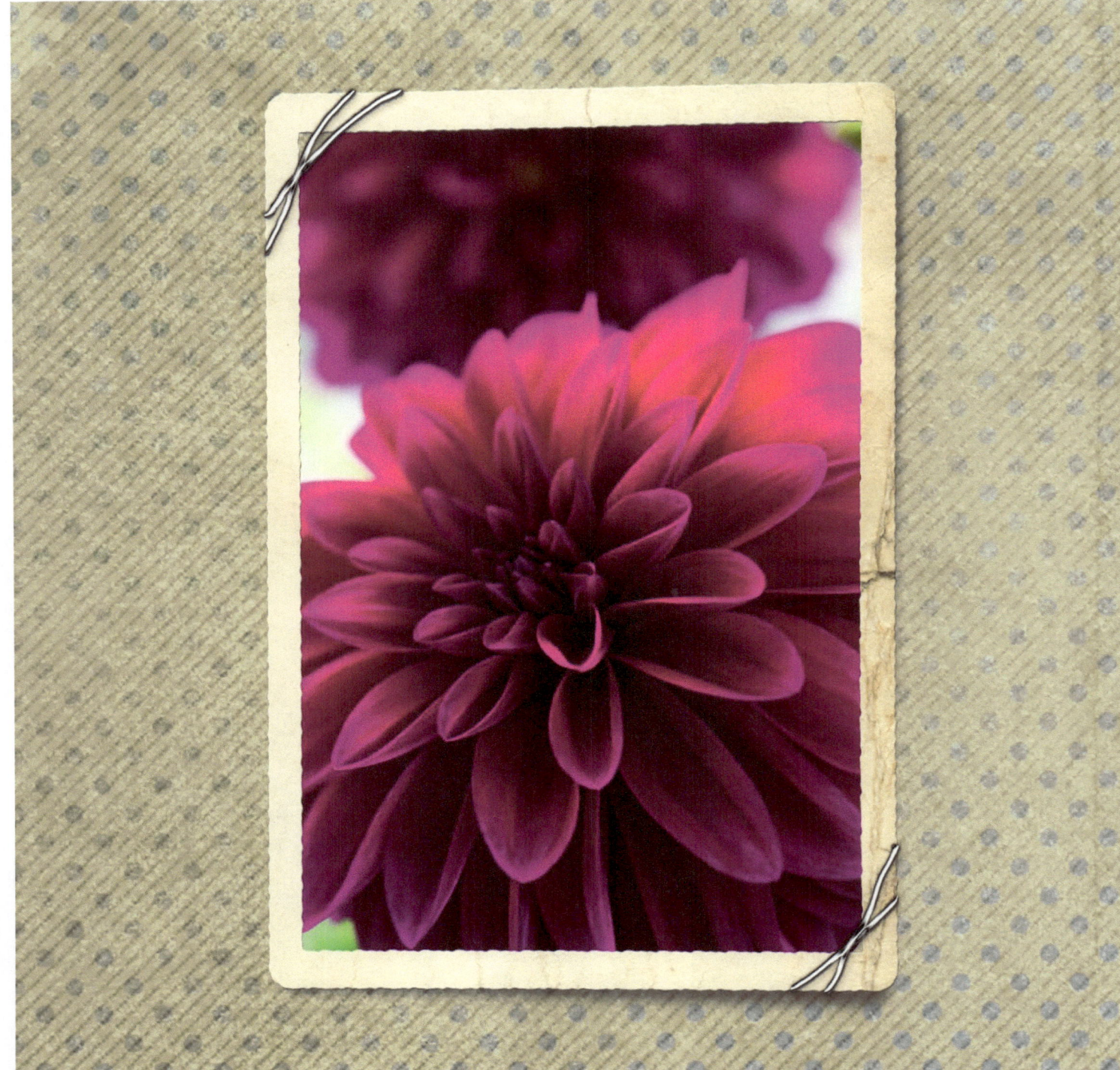

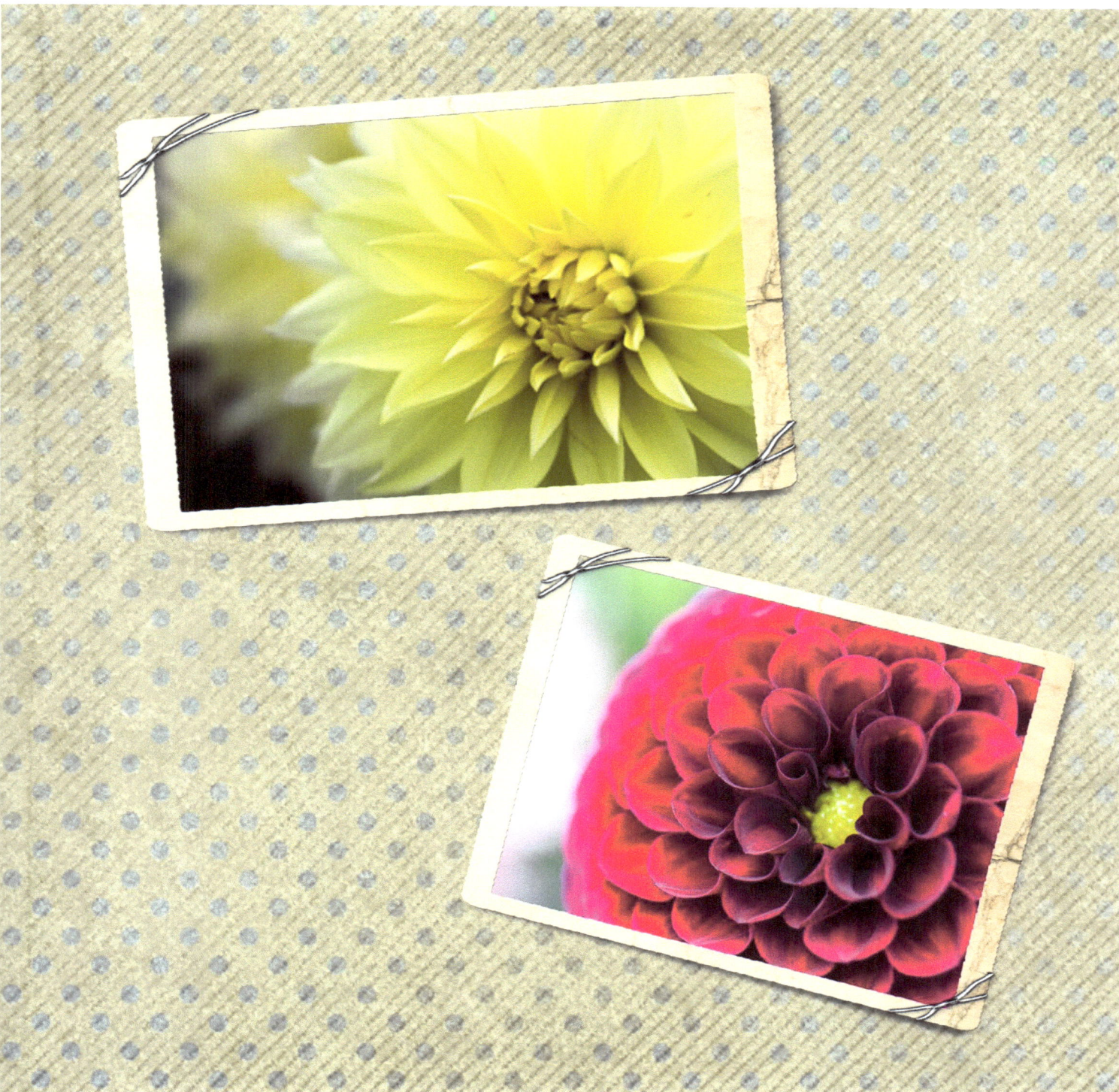

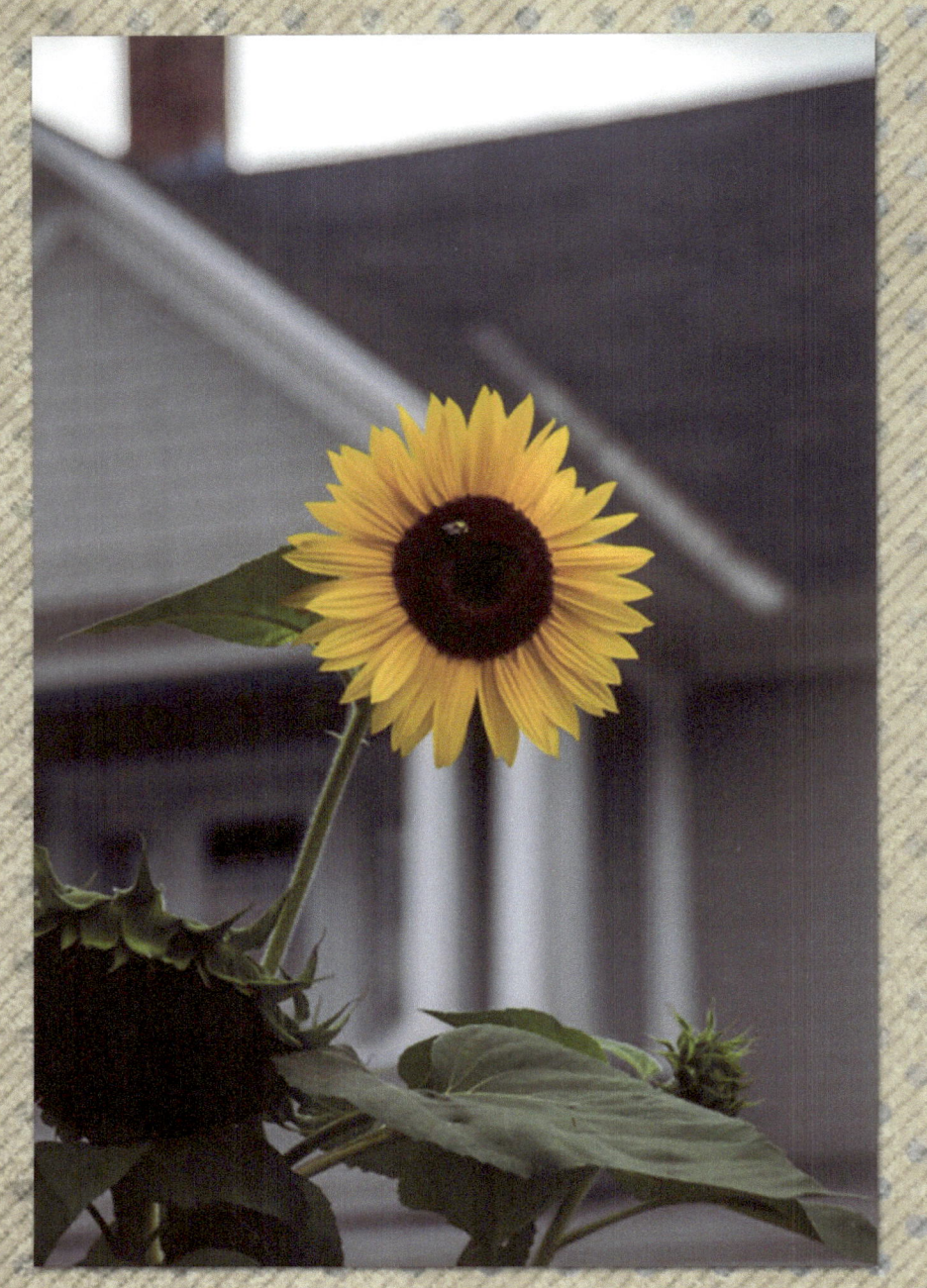

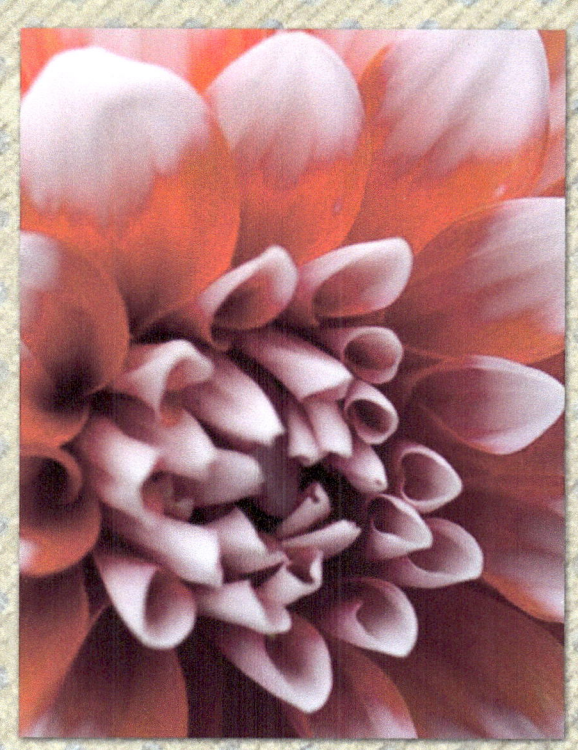

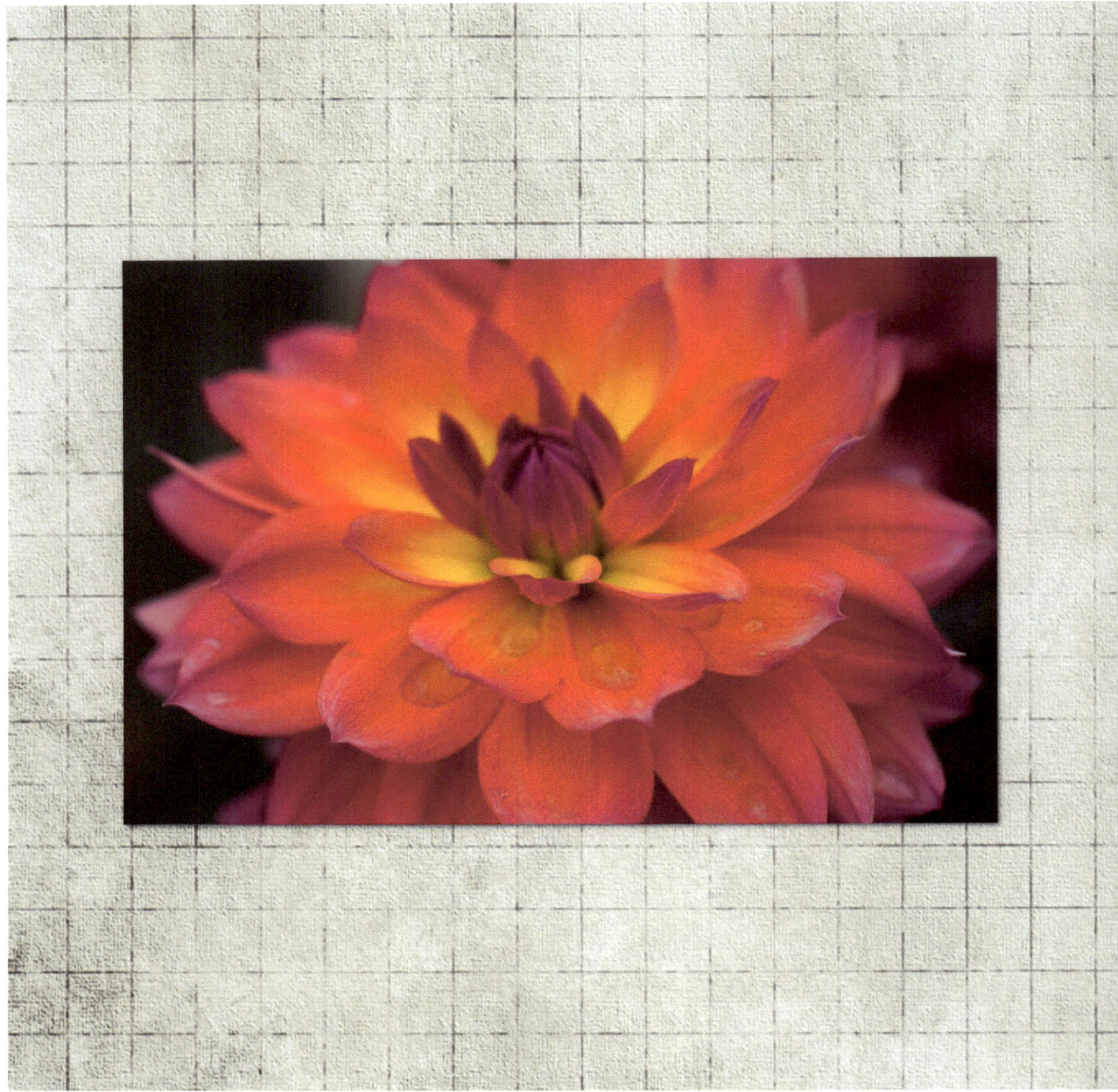

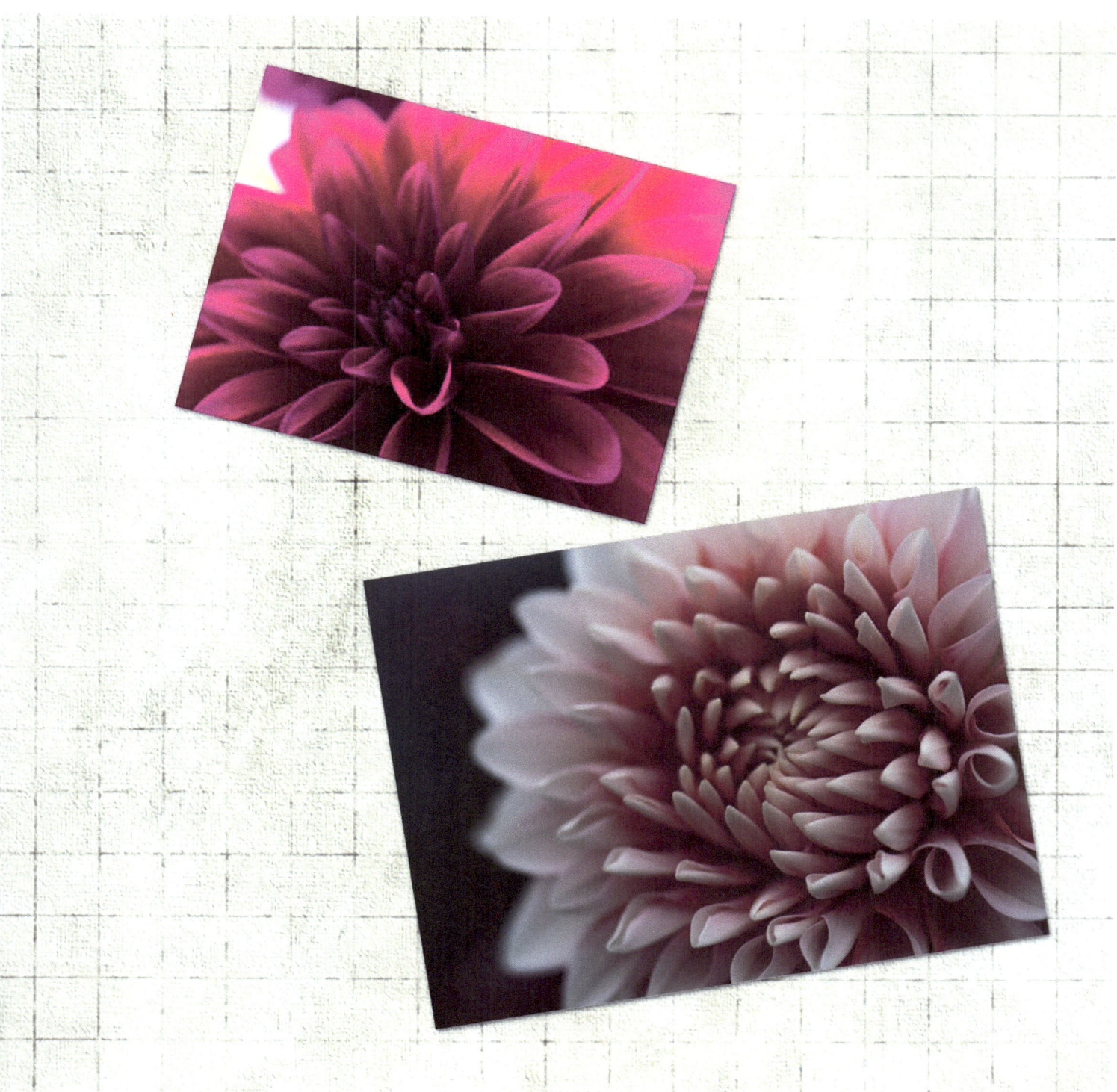

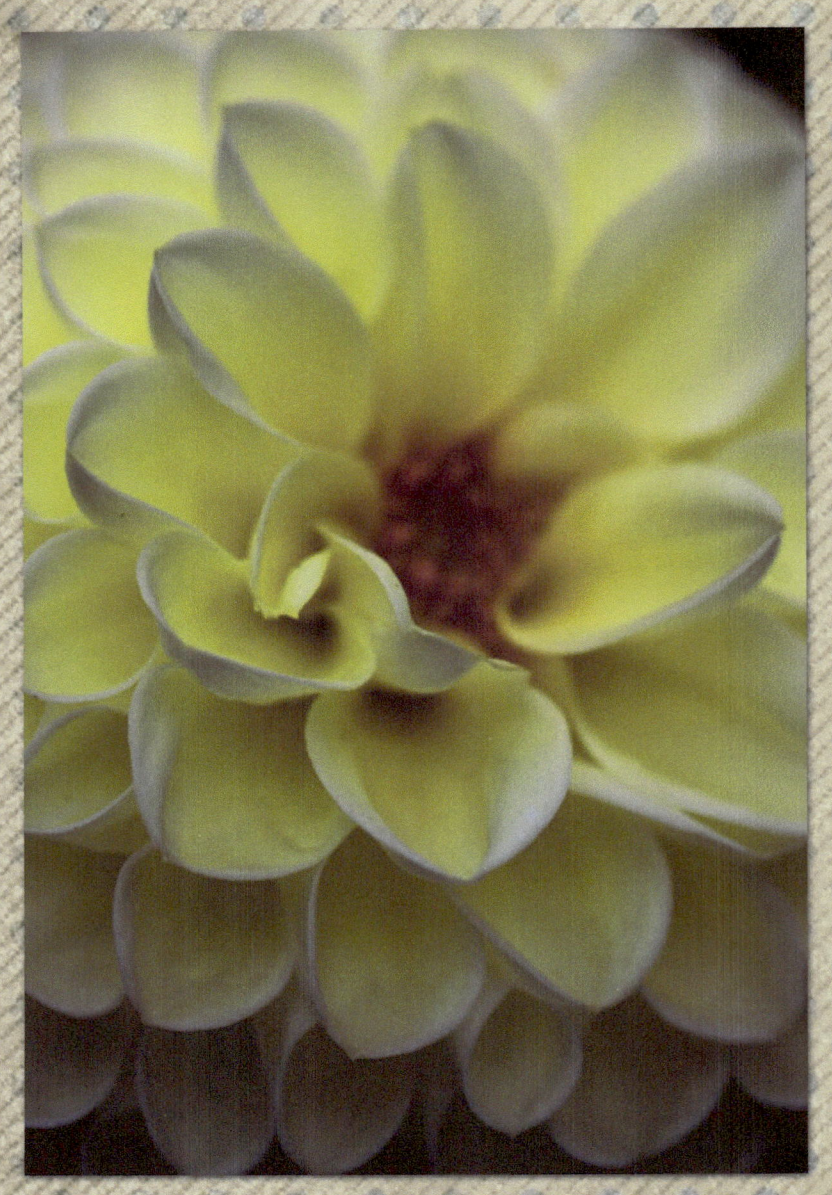

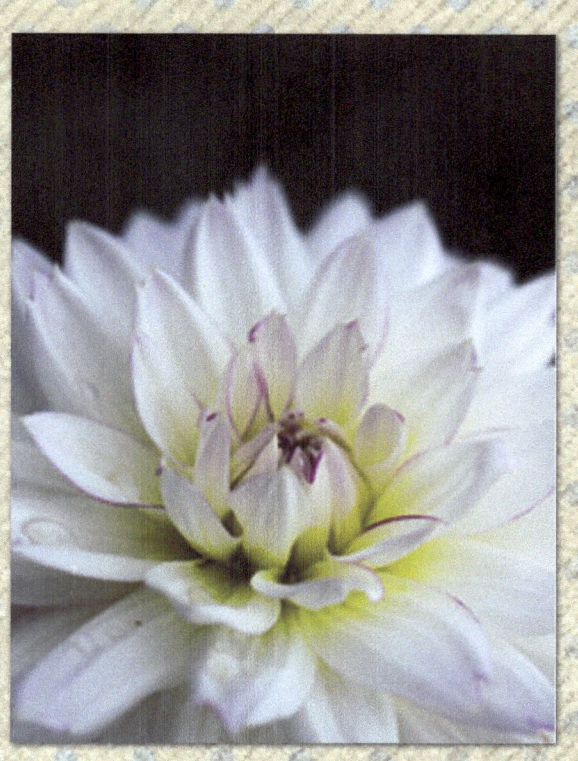
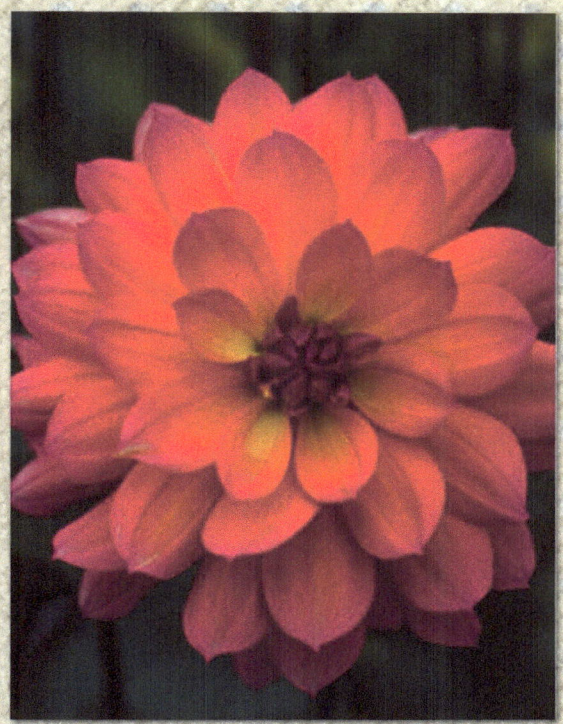

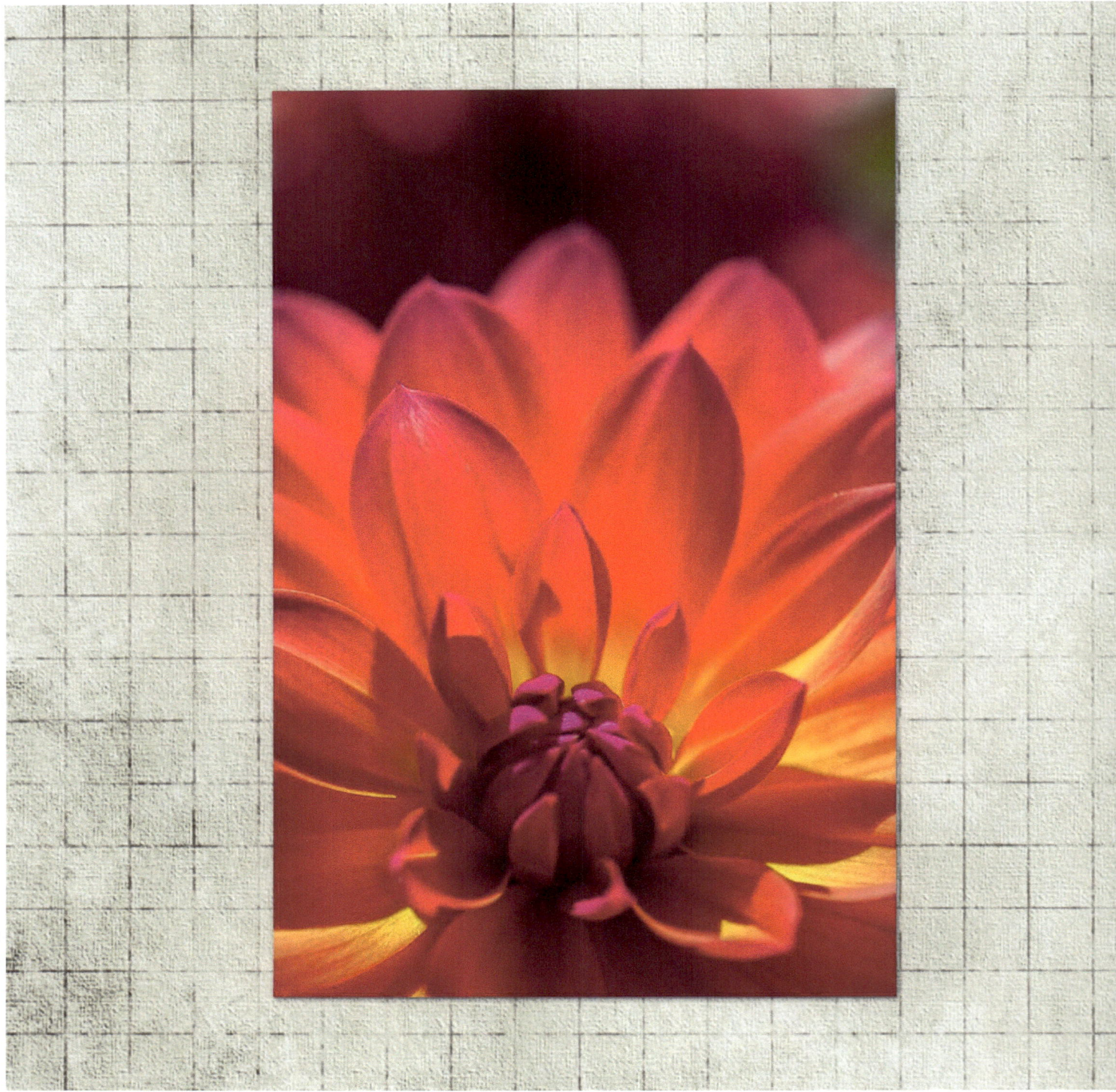

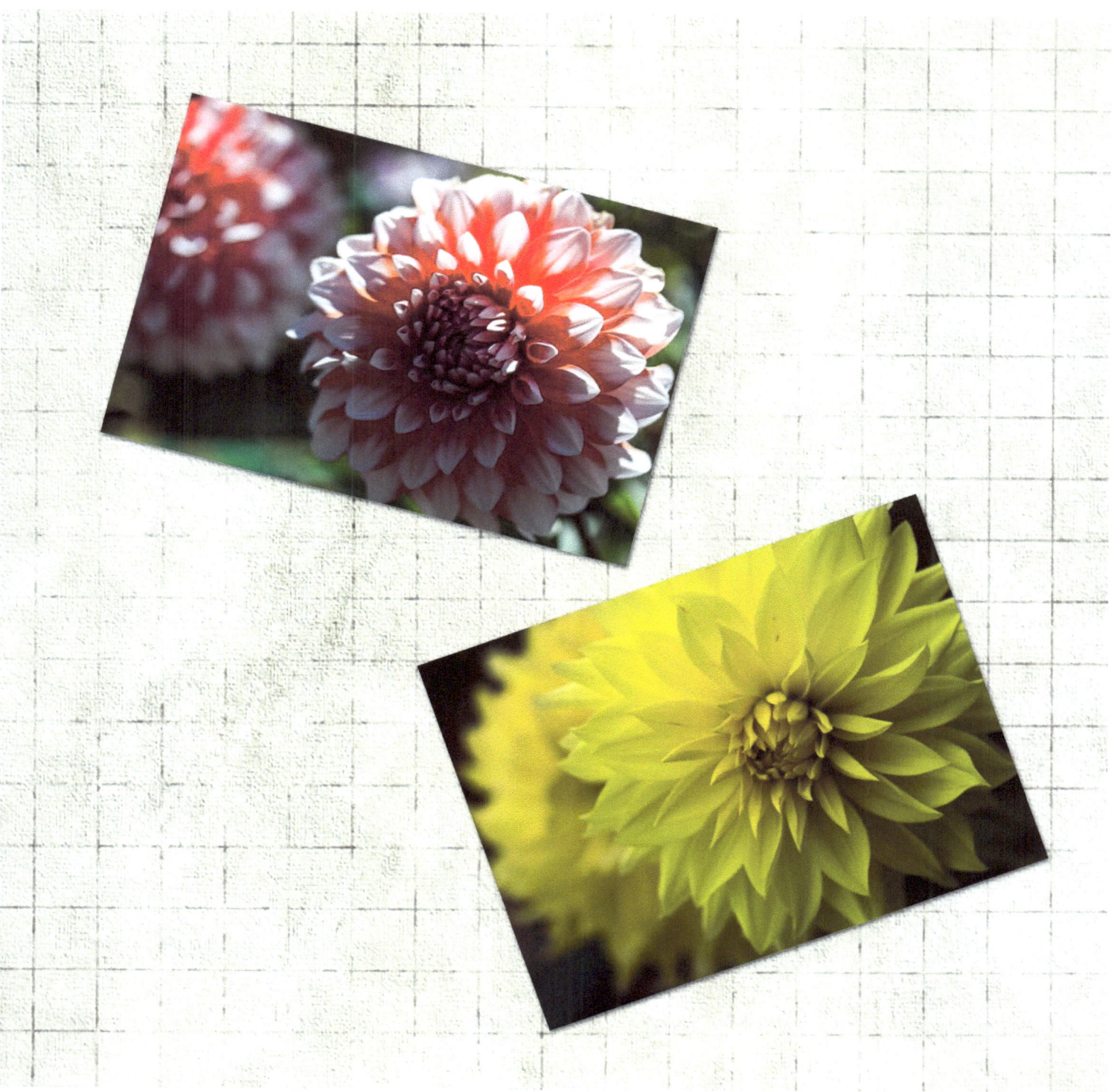

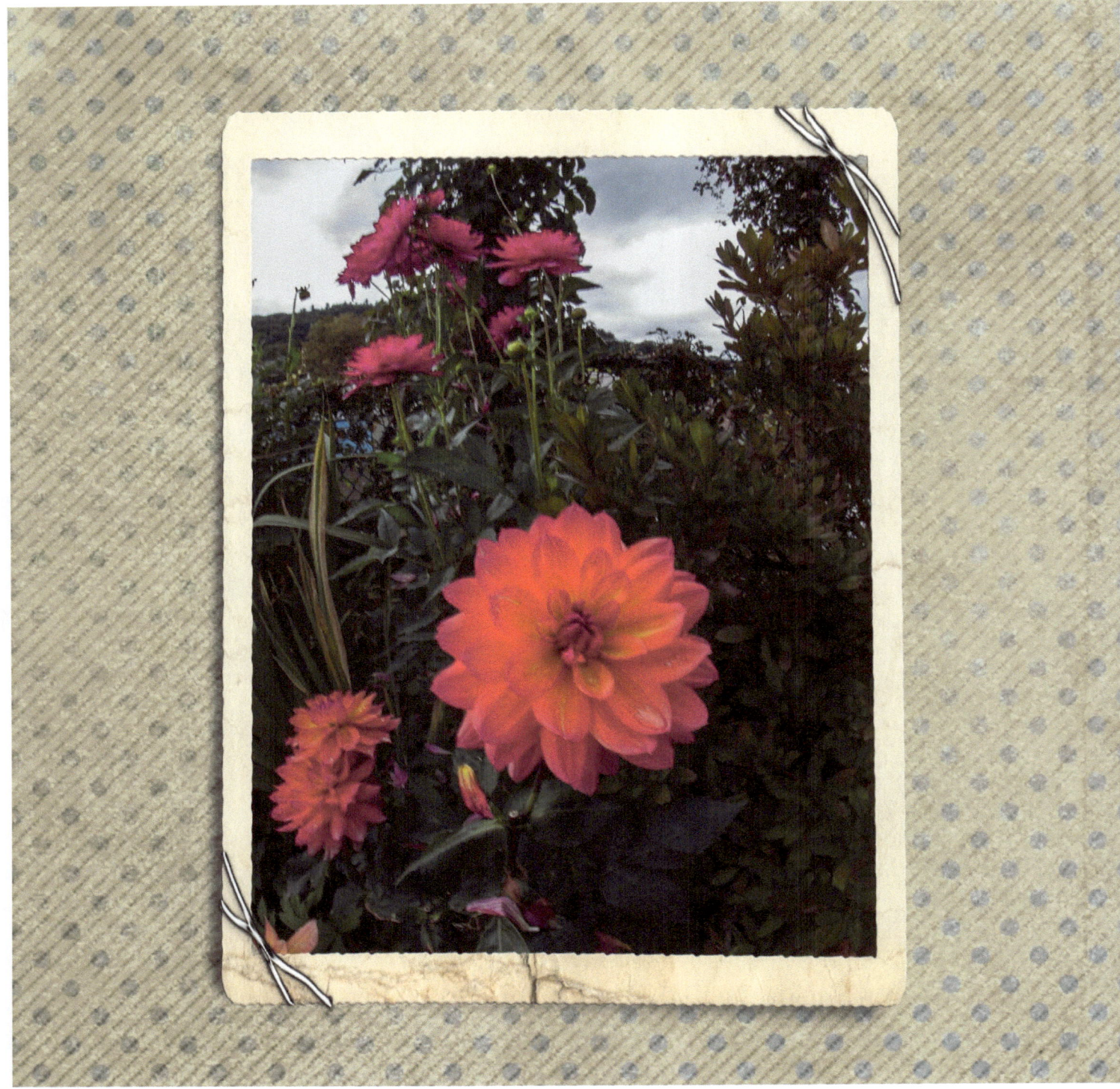

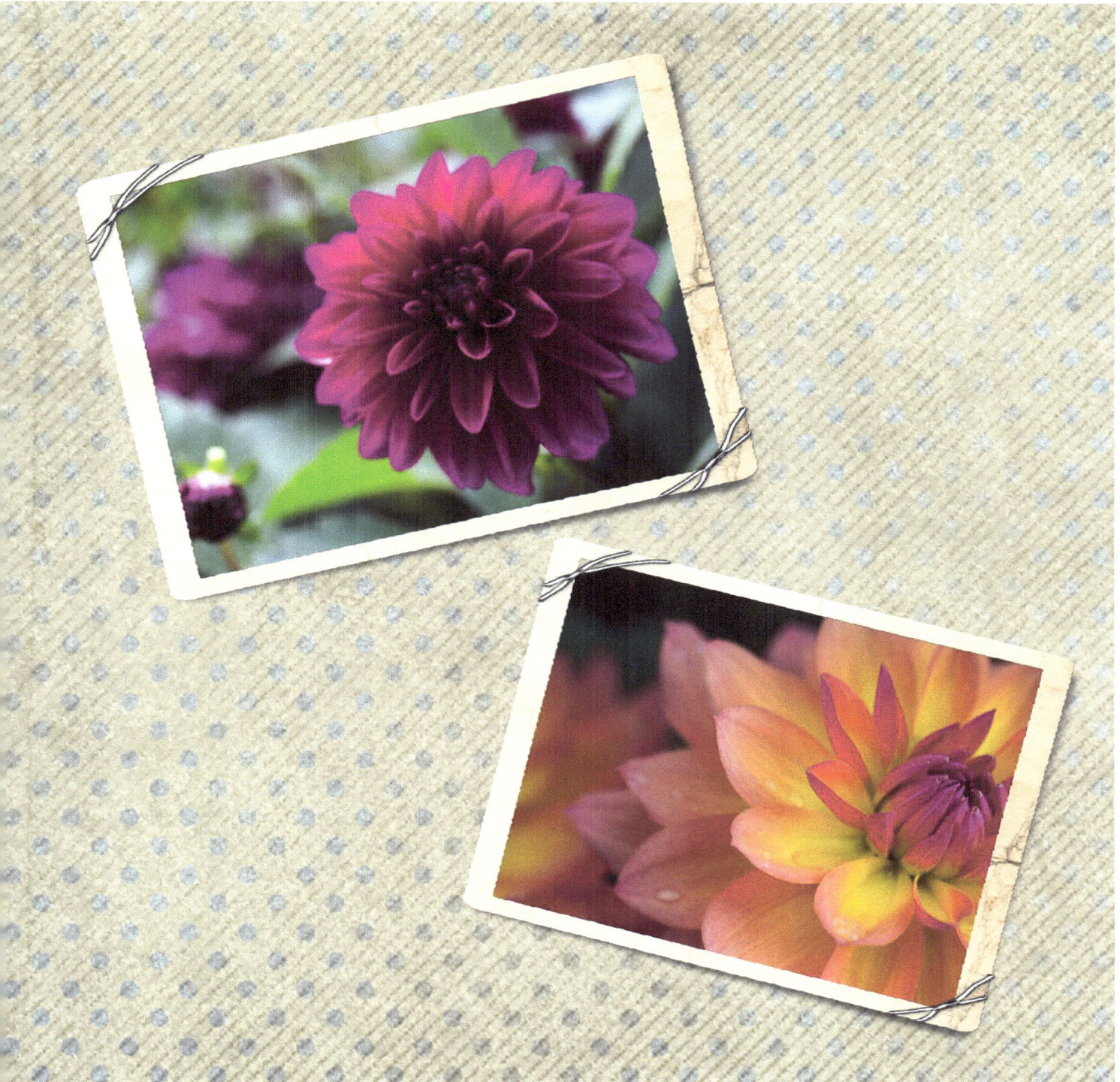

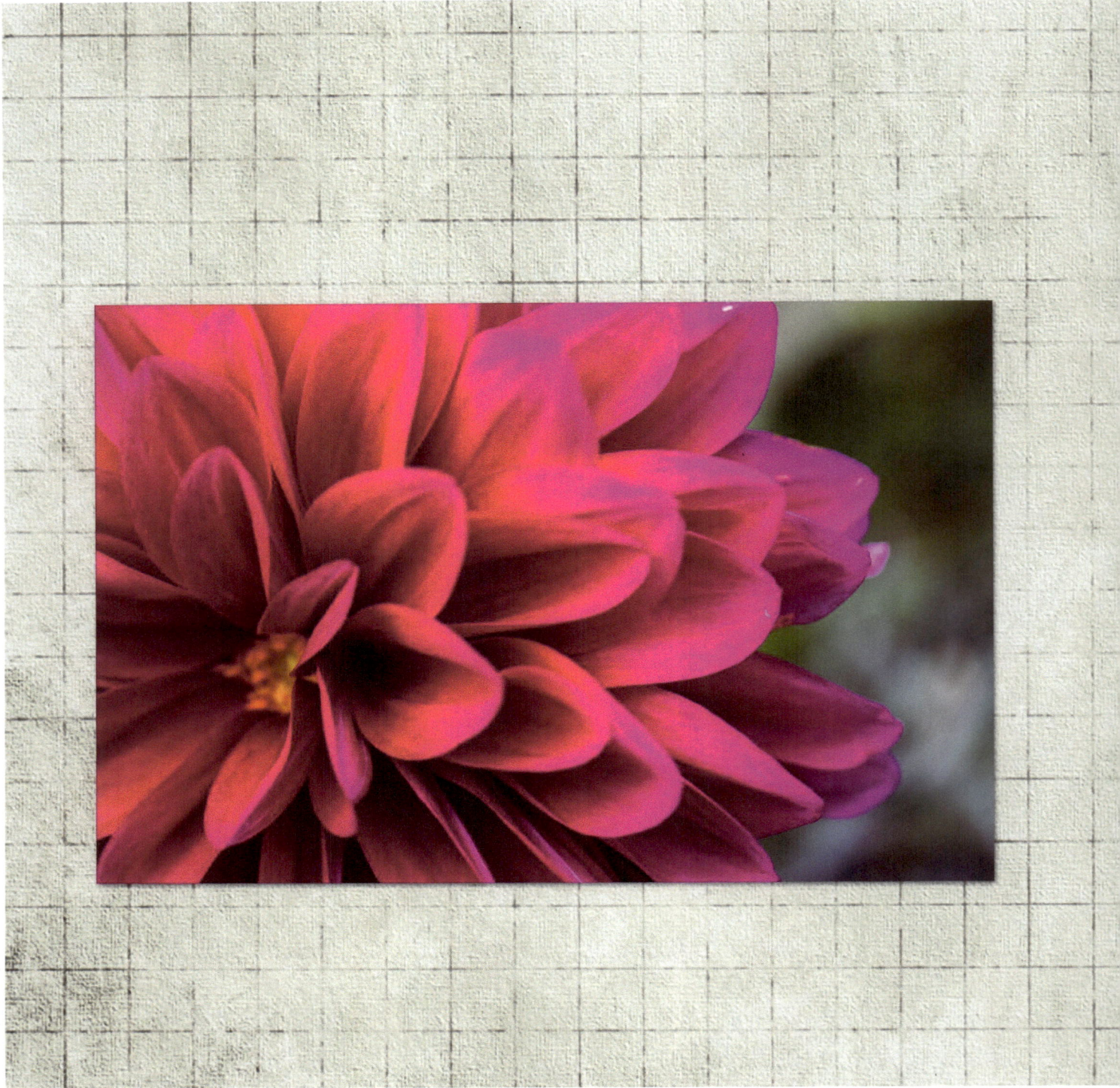

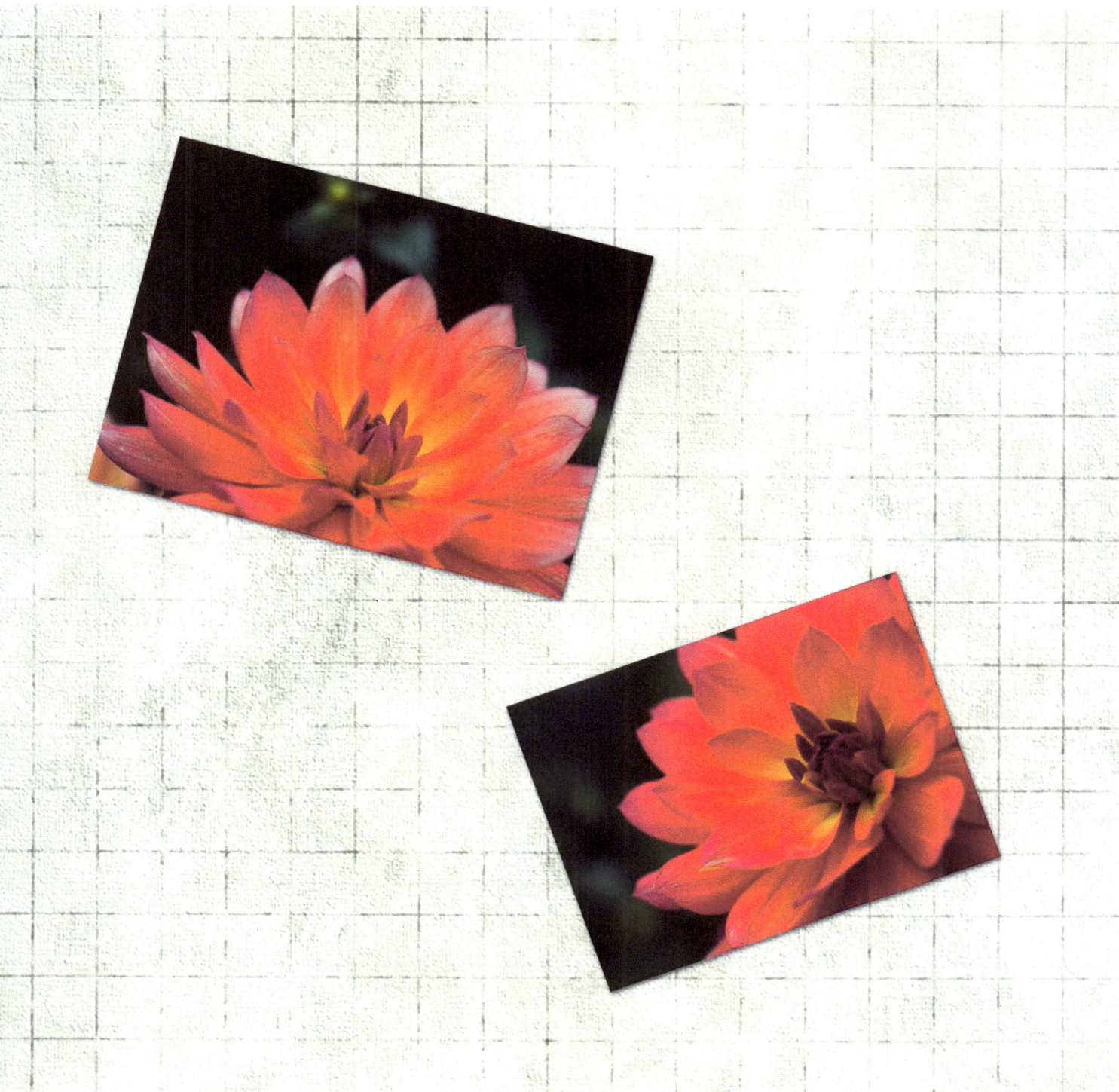

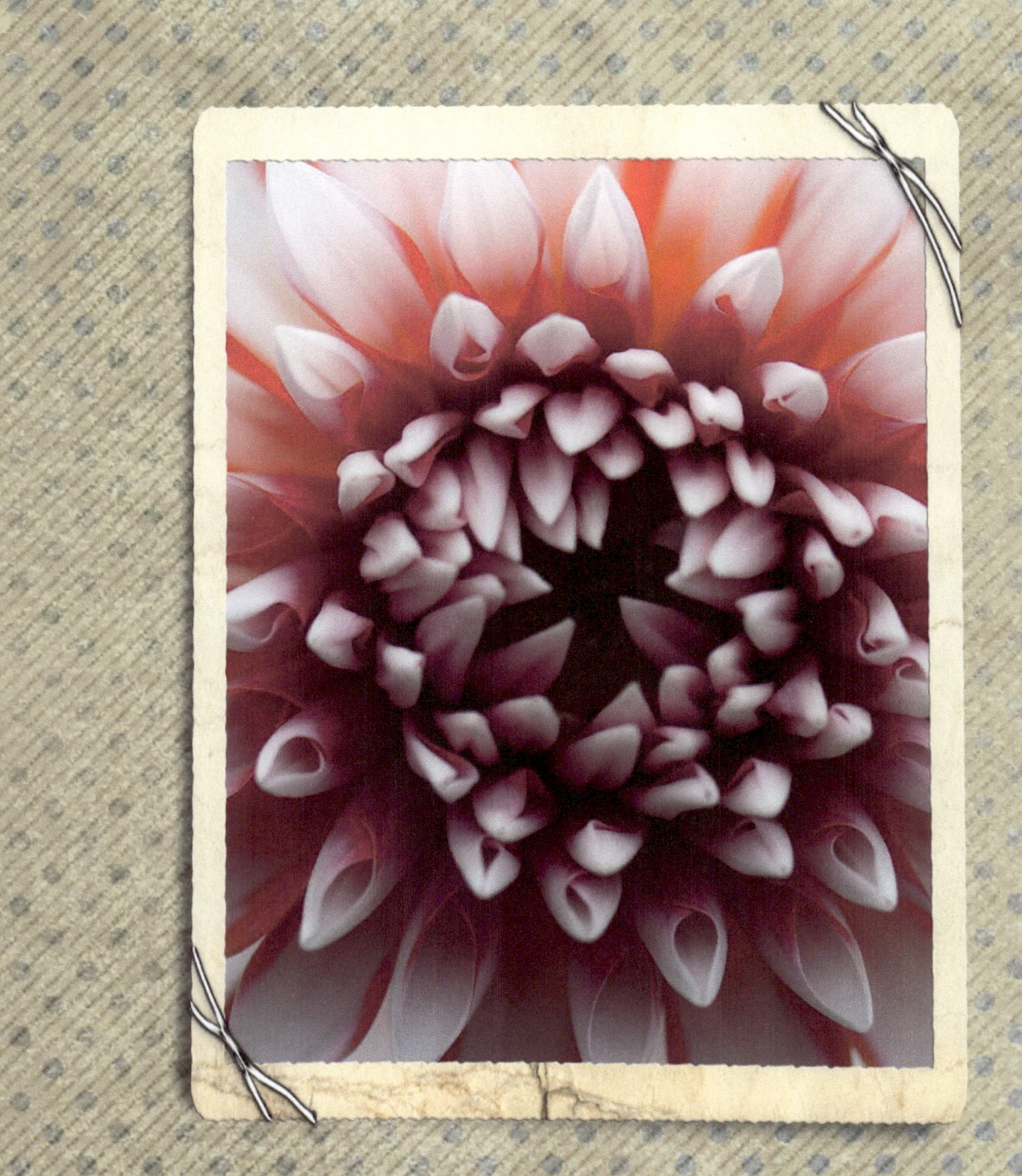

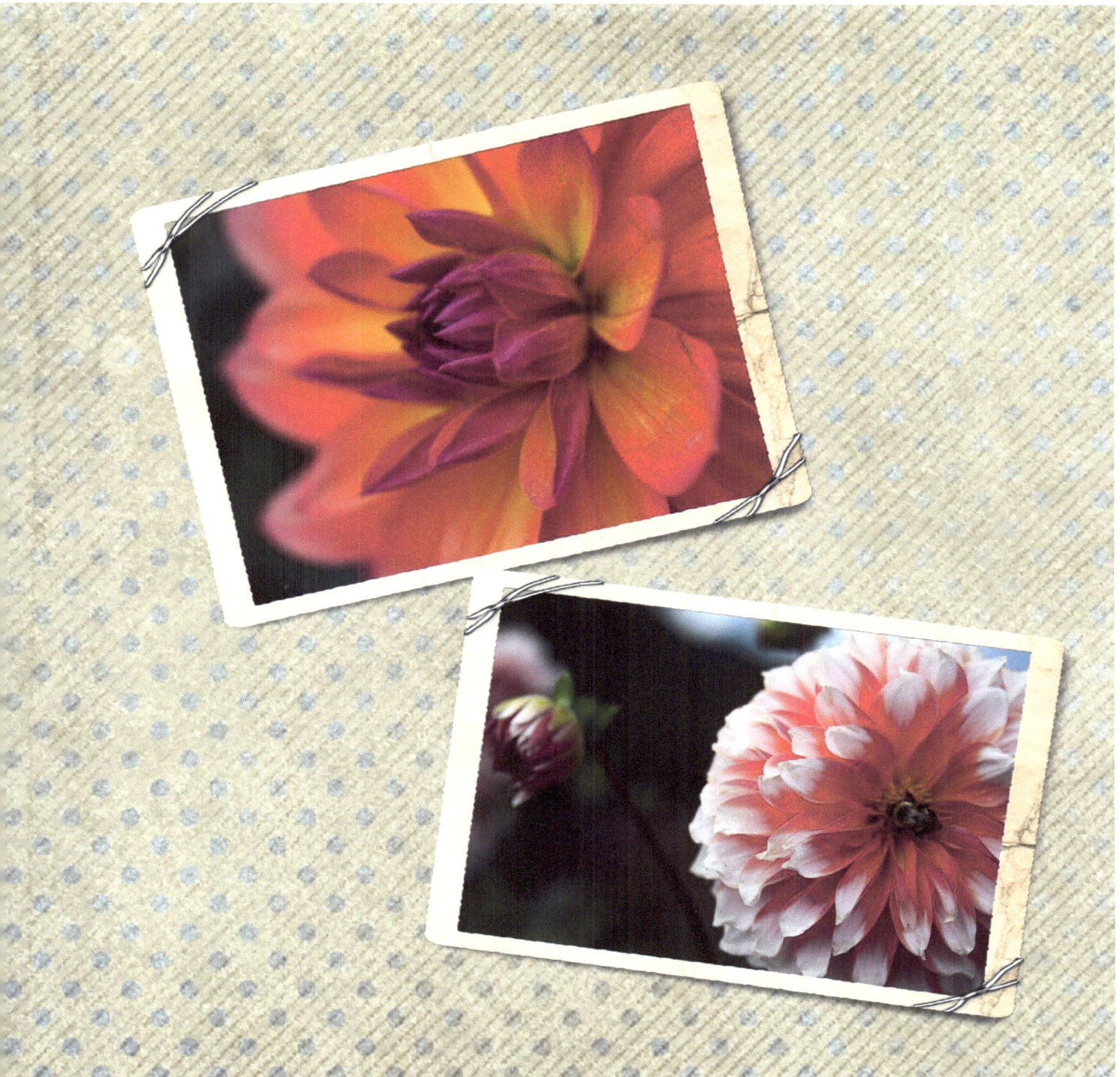

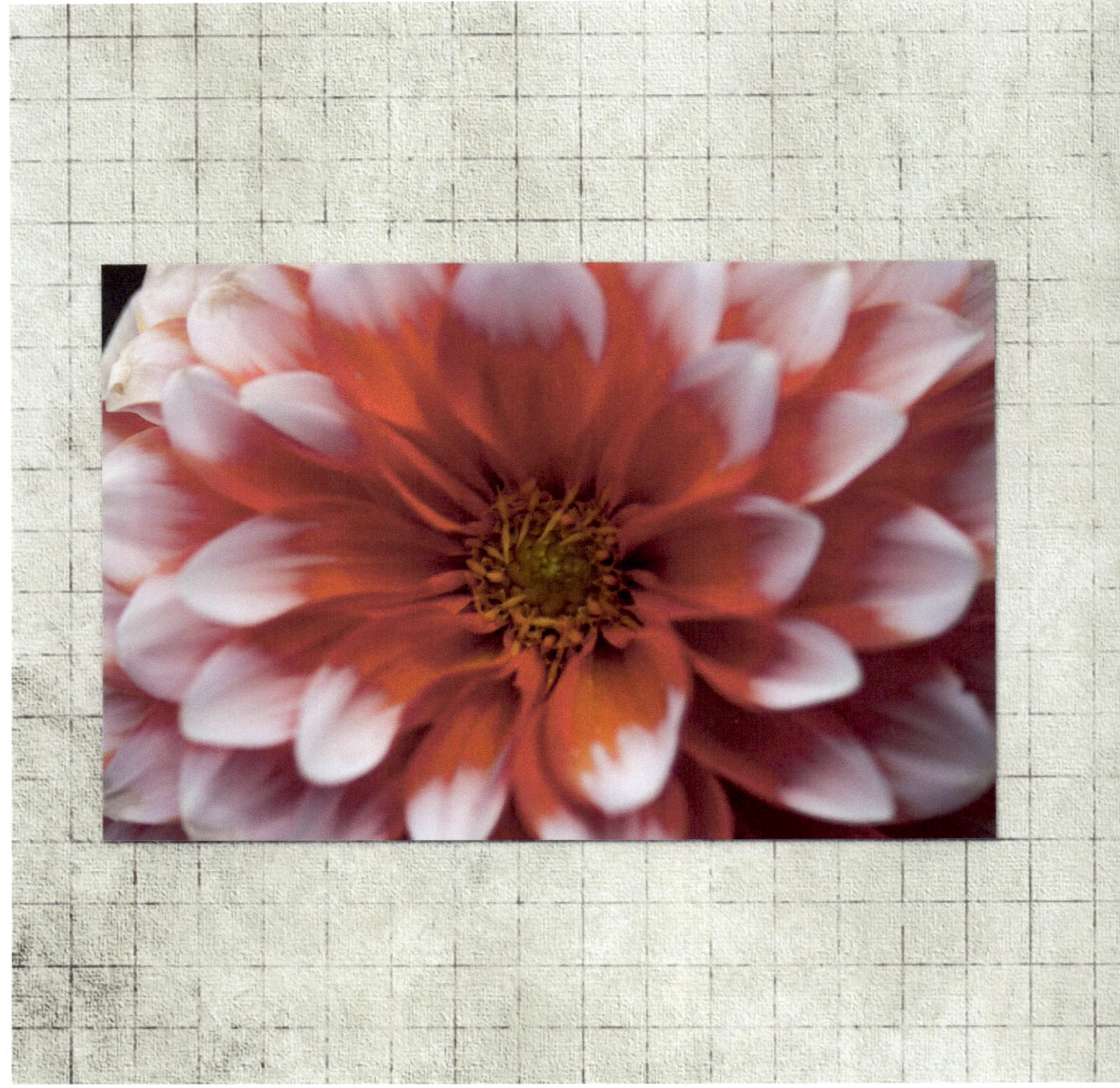

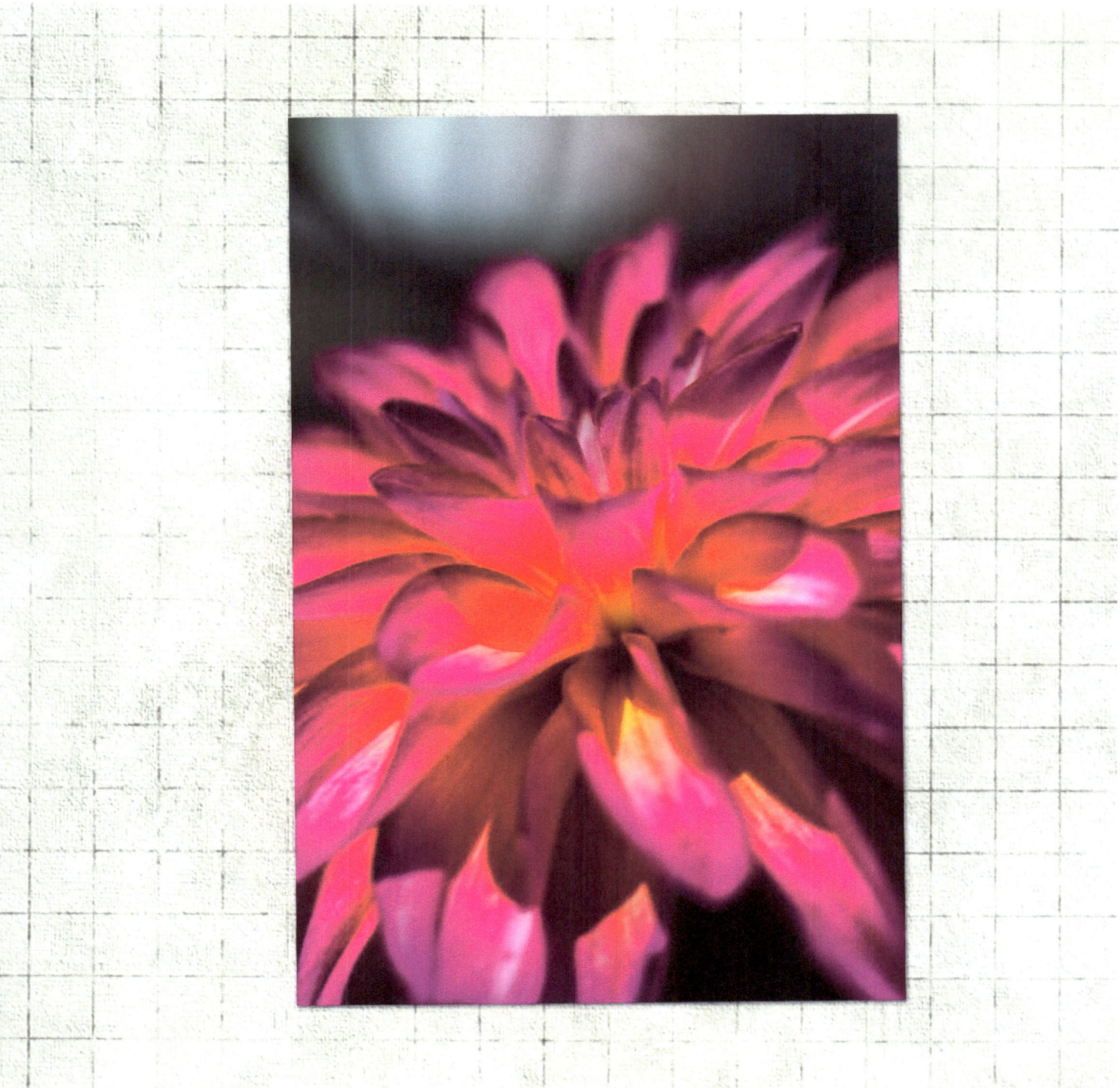

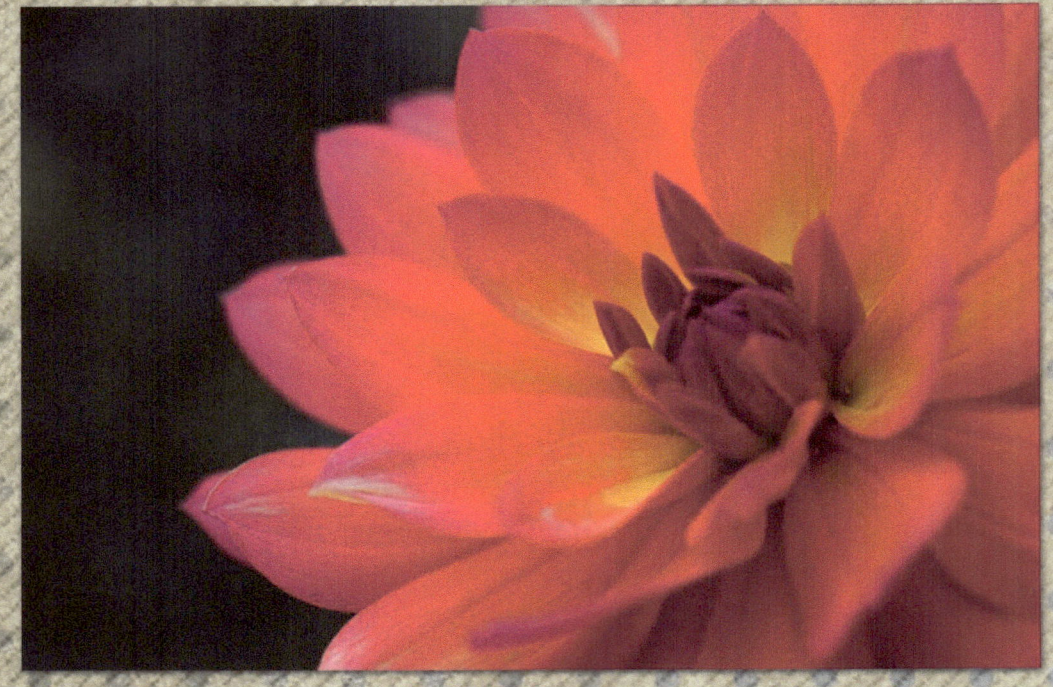

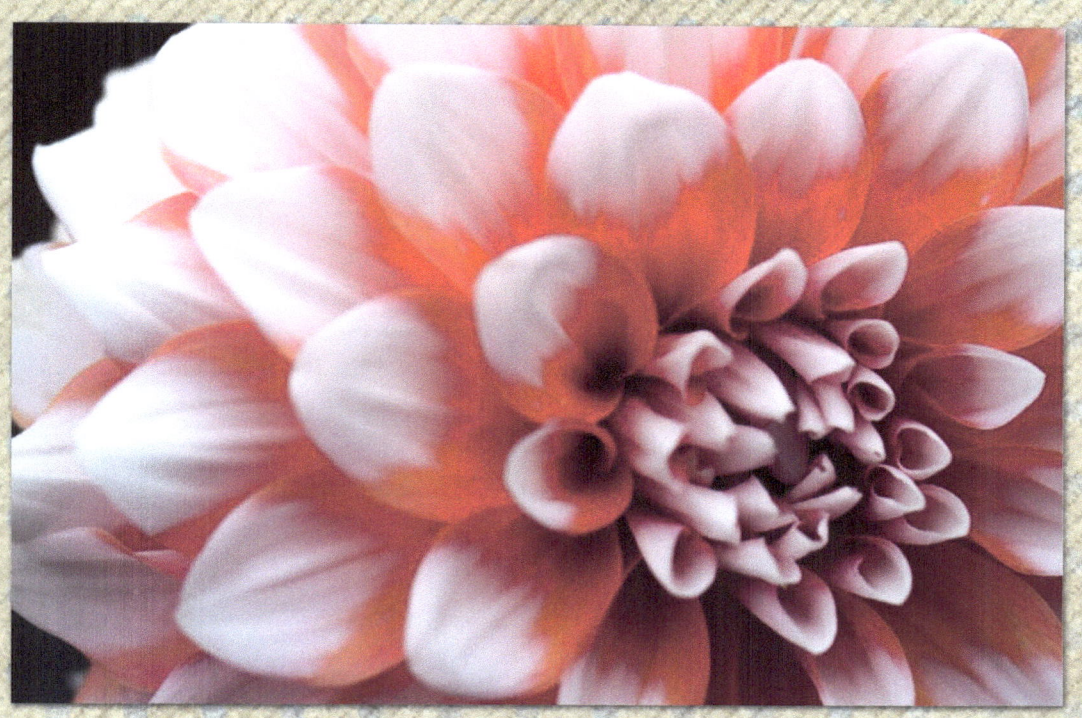

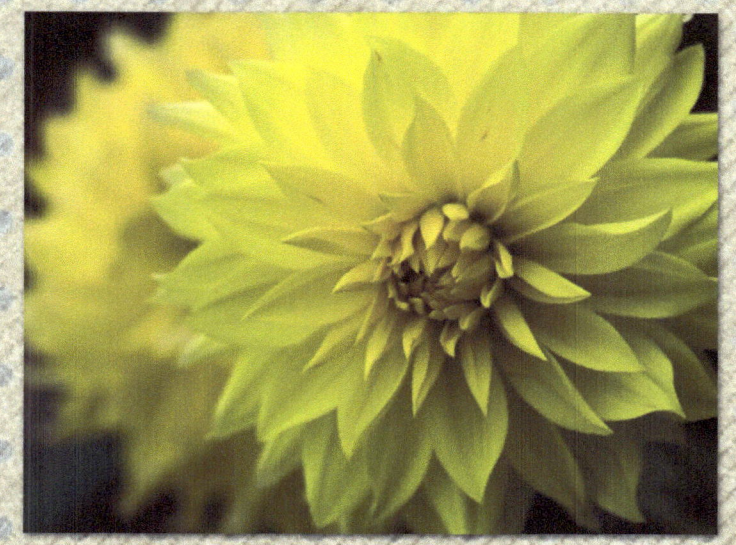

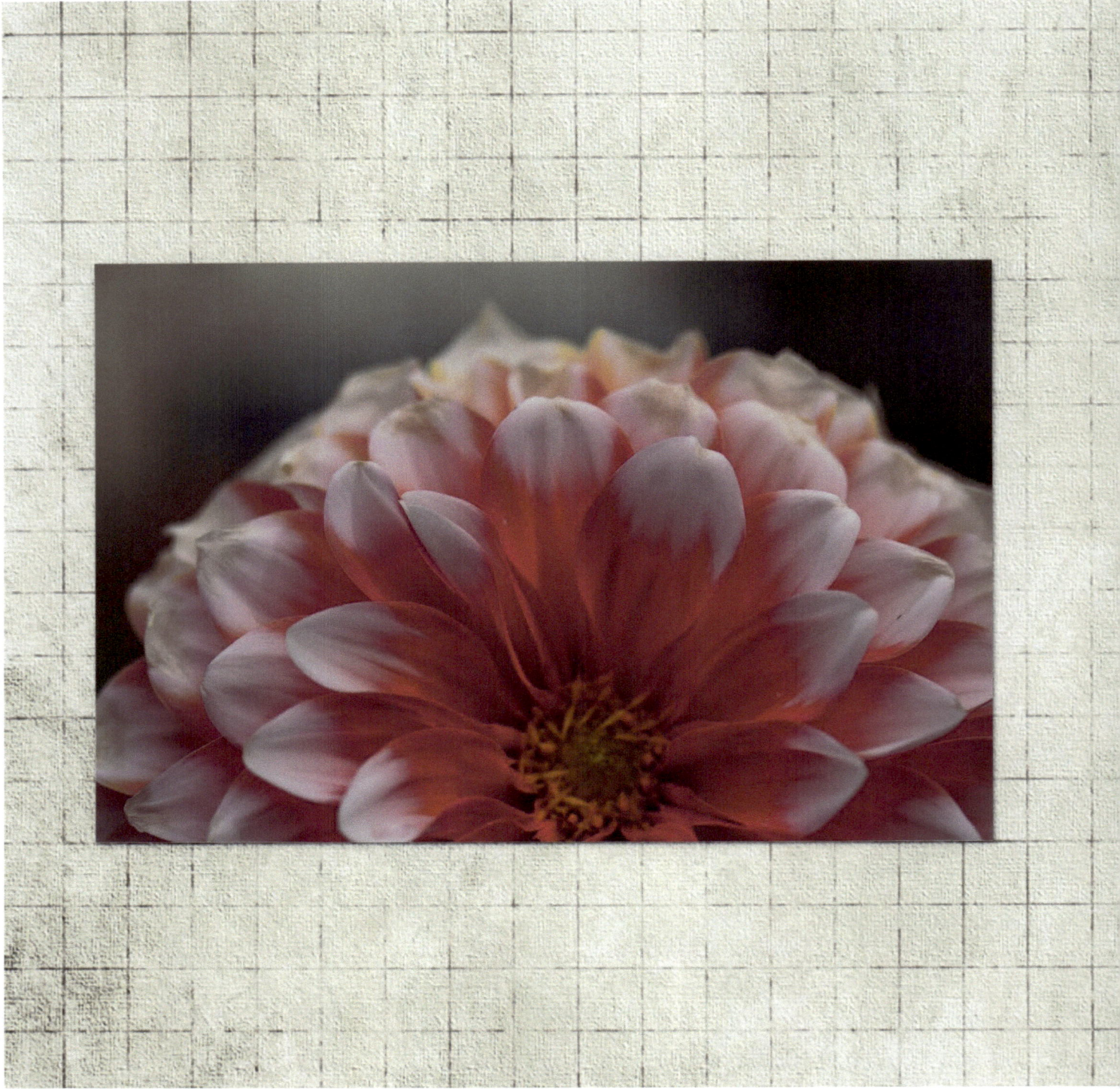

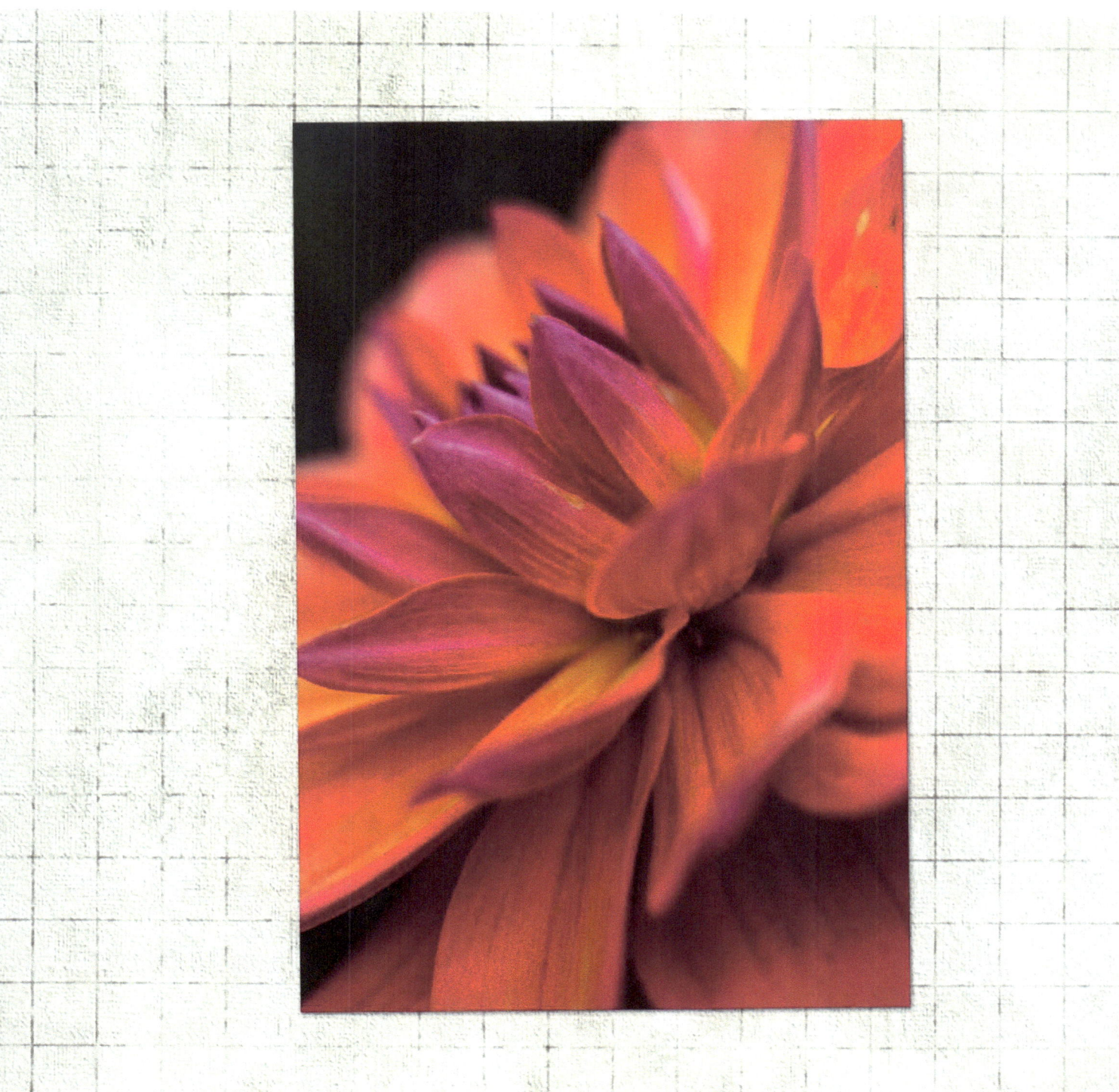

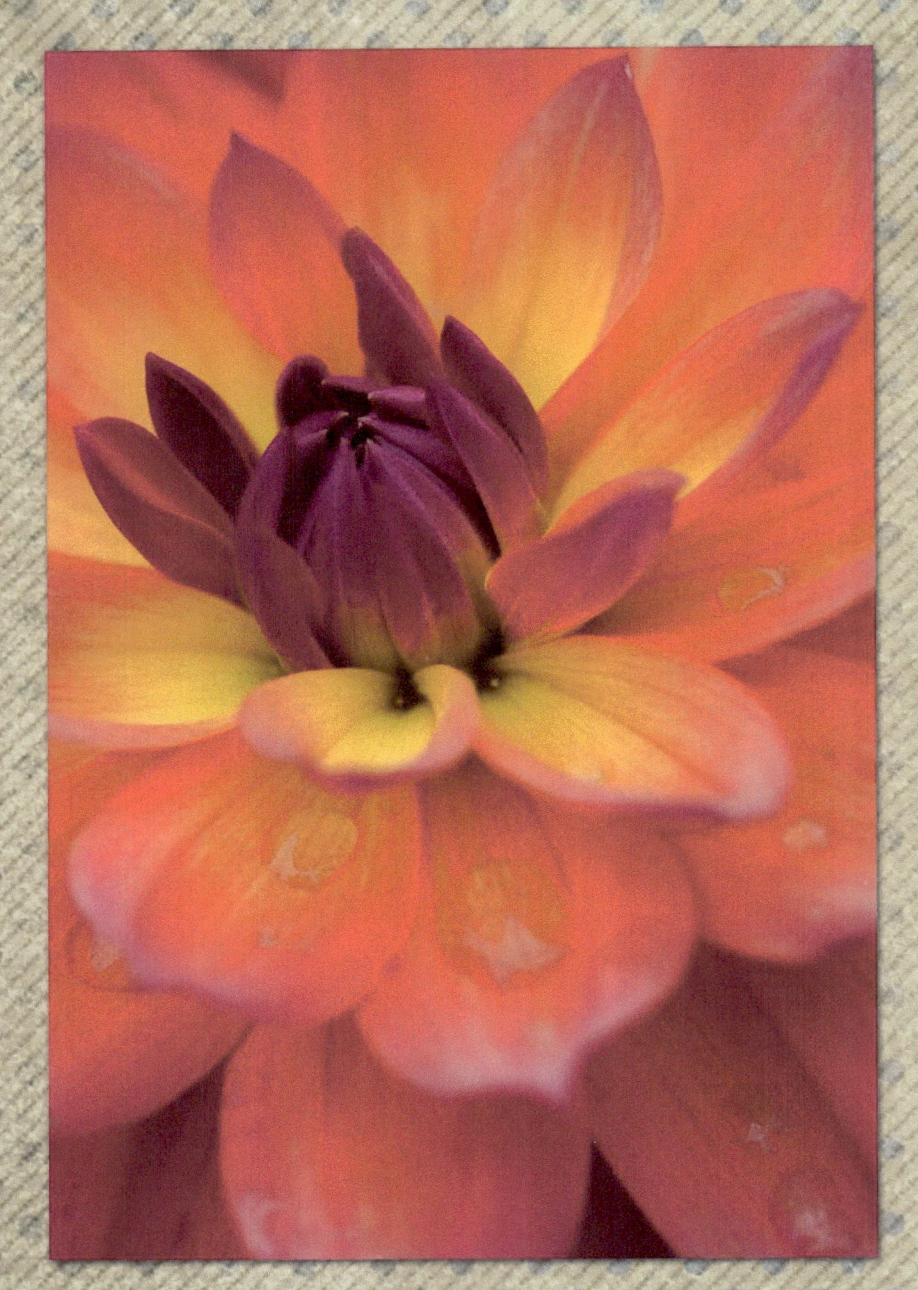

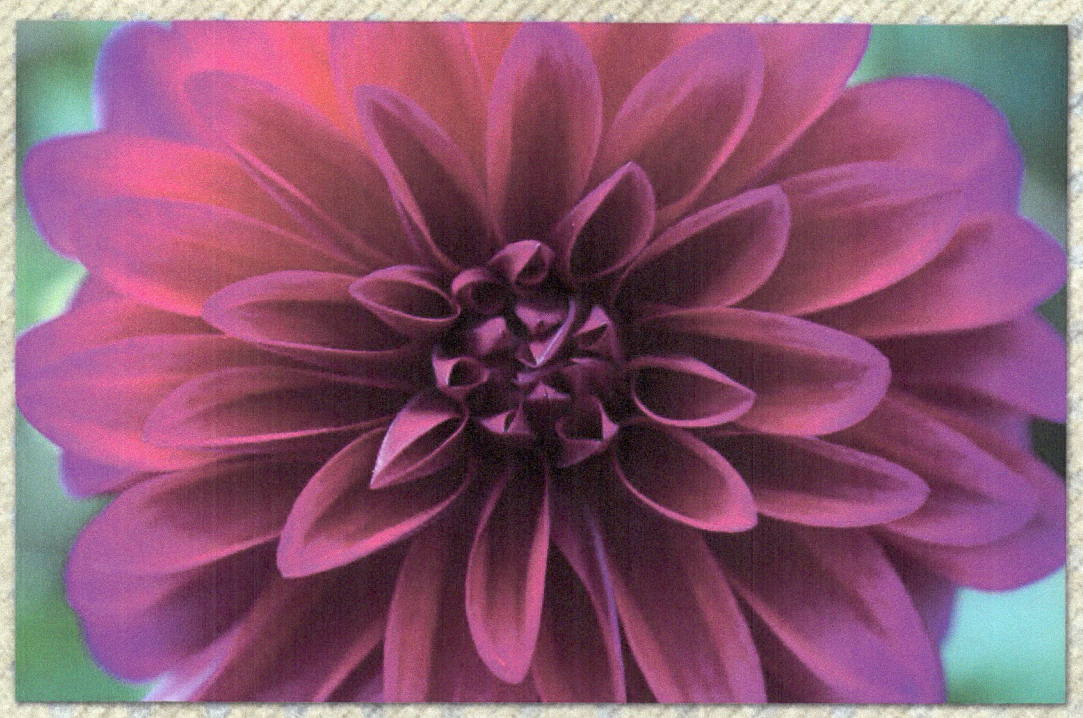

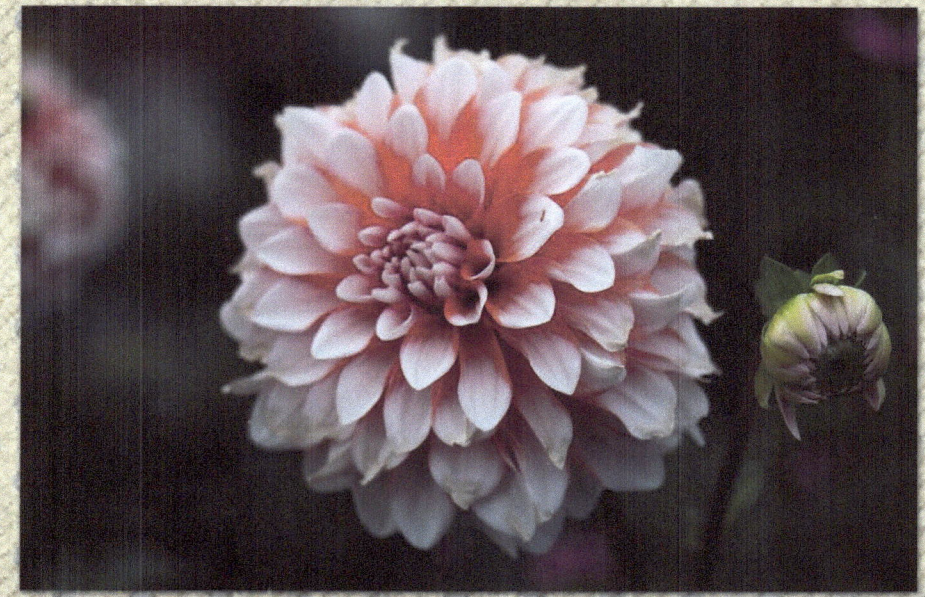

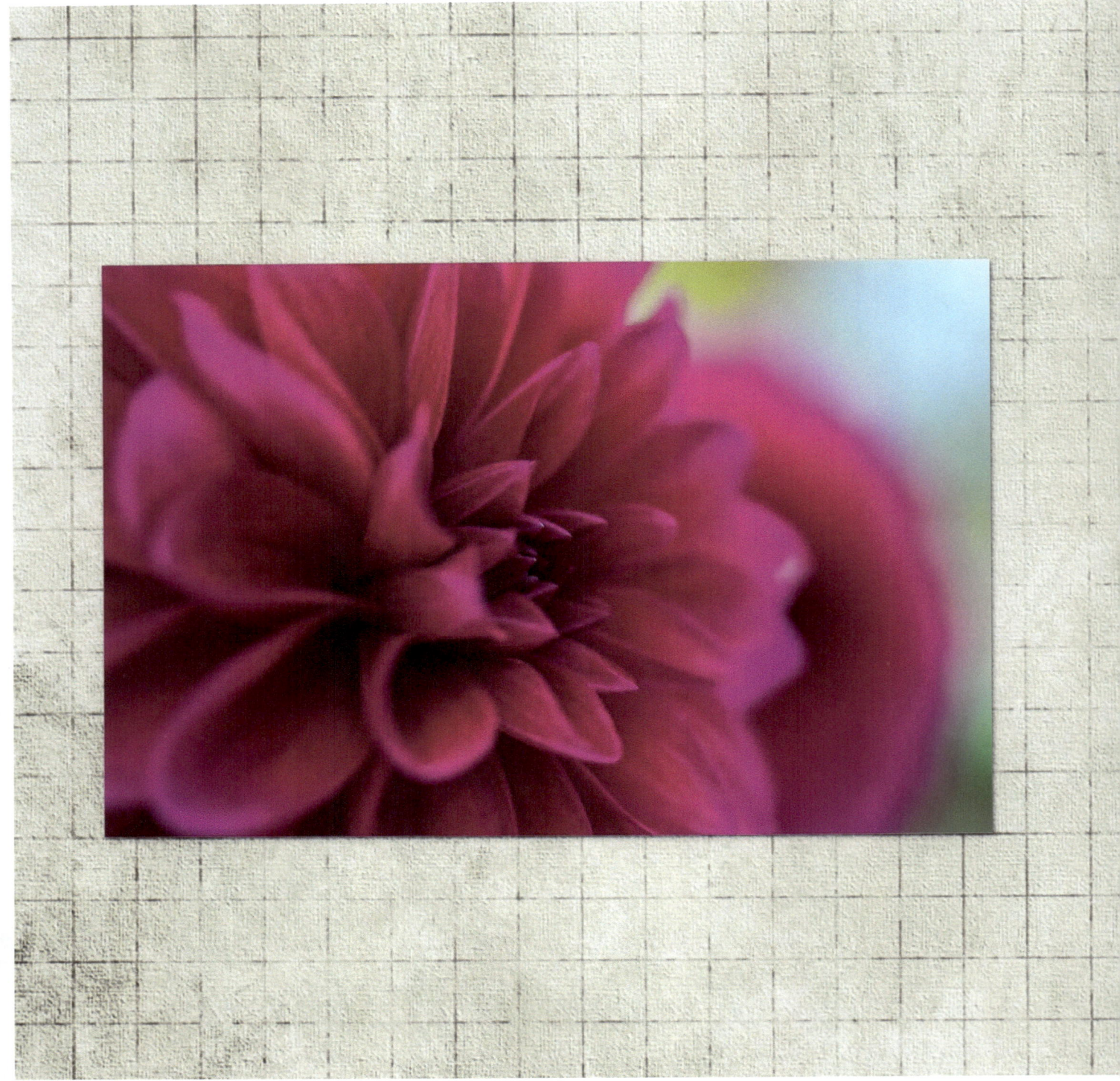